Angel on a Leash

Therapy Dogs and the Lives They Touch

by David Frei

BOWTIE
P R E S S®
A Division of BowTie, Inc.

Lead Editor: Amy Deputato
Senior Editor: Jarelle S. Stein
Design Manager: Véronique Bos
Art Director: Cindy Kassebaum
Production Supervisor: Jessica Jaensch
Assistant Production Manager: Tracy Vogtman
Book Project Specialist: Karen Julian

Vice President, Chief Content Officer: June Kikuchi
Vice President, Kennel Club Books: Andrew DePrisco
BowTie Press: Jennifer Calvert, Amy Deputato, Karen Julian,
Jarelle S. Stein

Front cover photos: Children and Teigh: Ronald McDonald House
New York/Neville Bean; Marine Lance Cpl. Joshua Bleill and Uno:
Mary Bloom; Heather Kingsbury and Angel: Mike Kingsbury; the
author and Angel: Danny Kim/*New York* Magazine. **Back cover
photo:** The author and Grace from the author's collection.

BowTie Press®
A Division of BOWTIE, INC.
3 Burroughs, Irvine, CA 92618

Library of Congress Cataloging-in-Publication Data

Frei, David.
  Angel on a leash : therapy dogs and the lives they touch / David
Frei.
     p. cm.
  ISBN 978-1-935484-63-9 (pbk.)
  1. Dogs--Therapeutic use--Anecdotes. 2. Working dogs--
Anecdotes. I. Title.
  RM931.D63F74 2011
  615.8'5158--dc23
                                        2011023964

Printed and bound in Canada
17 16 15 14 13 12 11   2 3 4 5 6 7 8 9 10

Dedication

To Teigh, Belle, Angel, and Grace,
for letting me be the guy on the other end of the leash.

To Jessie,
for her courage and her full-speed approach to life.

To Andrea,
for her quiet dignity and her ever-present smile.

And to Mom.
Just because.

Contents

Foreword

by John O'Hurley

Dogs bring out the good in good people. No one told me that. It's just an observation that I've made after wandering deeper into the canine world and witnessing the extraordinary impact that dogs have on the world around them. I have written before that I am a better person with a dog in my lap, and I believe that more today than when I first put that thought to paper.

But I probably would have missed that thought as well as the deeper meaning of how dogs enrich our lives had I not answered a phone call nearly ten years ago. The call was from one of the executives at NBC Sports who began the conversation with the words, "Woof, woof." He went on to explain that they were taking a chance and developing a dog show to air on Thanksgiving Day called the National Dog Show presented by Purina. He asked if I would host the show along with a gentleman he described as "the most knowledgeable mind in the world of dogs." That tag still applies to David Frei. I said yes to the offer to host and began a tremendous and enduring friendship with David and his wife Cheri. That friendship introduced me and my wife Lisa not only to a deeper understanding of the commitment and responsibility of dog ownership but also to a deeper and more spiritual purpose for dogs as companions in medical and emotional therapy.

Through his Angel On A Leash organization, I have seen firsthand the good that therapy dogs do—in the cancer wards and in pediatrics. A dog's simple presence brings an irreplaceable moment of stillness and levity to the ill and the elderly. I have watched the hollow look of a sick child turn to a twinkle and smile when a therapy dog leaps on the child's bed.

When a dog wags his tail, it is connected to his heart. When David tells these stories of the dogs he has known and the good that they've done, they are connected to his.

I leave you in good hands.

Acknowledgments

This story isn't about me. It's about all of these great dogs and people who do good things for others every single day. They are the dogs and people of my world, and they have made this book come to life. I have so many of them to thank.

First, my wonderful wife, Cherilyn, on this road with me, the person who has taught me so much about life and about myself and my dogs and the great things that they can do and that we can do together.

My dogs, Teigh and Belle—God rest their orange-and-white souls—and Angel and Grace, who are carrying on for them.

The breeders who brought these four-legged angels into my life: Jeane White, Patty Kanan, Cindy Huggins, Linda McCartney-Roy, and Kristyn McCartney; the veterinarians who have cared for them: Dr. Jean Dodds, Dr. Meghan Myott, Dr. Jamie Warren, Dr. Nicole Buote, Dr. Janet Kovak, Dr. Cara Horowitz, and a bunch of others at the Animal Medical Center; and the people who help us care for them daily (dog walkers and dog sitters): Emily Key, Althea Alvarez, Maria Angeles, Doug Tighe, and my in-laws, Emily and Lyle Smith.

Christi Dudzik, my mentor in therapy dog work, my vice chairman of the Angel On A Leash board, and, more importantly, my friend; and my special friends Wayne Ferguson, Larry Leib, Tom Lasley, Ranny Green, and Chris Terrell, always there for me.

Those very special Westminster Best in Show dogs,

Uno, James, and Rufus, and their owners, Caroline Dowell, Terry Patton, and Tom and Barbara Bishop; also, Ceil Ruggles, Scott Sommer, Eddie Dziuk, Dan Huebner, and Aaron Wilkerson.

My leaders and colleagues at the Westminster Kennel Club: Peter Van Brunt, Tom Bradley, Chet Collier, Florence Foti, Kelly Rounds, Billy Mott, Linda Duane, and Sharon Fremer.

All of the Angel On A Leash people: Greer Griffith, Christine DeAcetis, Nancy George-Michalson, Mary Ehrhart, Stephanie LaFarge, Chuck Bessant, Richard Dienst, Barbara Babikian, Caroline Loevner, Gay Cropper, and all of the teams that visit in our facilities; and great Angel supporters Karen LeFrak, Susan Stone, Ann Howie, Val Diker, Ruth Pereira, Joe Yanek, Ron Trotta and Elly McGuire, Kristina Newman, Eric Gural, Debra Vey Voda-Hamilton, Michele Siegel, Dr. Race Foster and Dr. Marty Smith, Gordon Magee, Mary Bloom, Toni Millar, Maggie Butterfield, Catherine DiPasquale, Peggy Schunk, Bill Sullivan, Jim Murray, Wendy Gallart, Frank Kelley, Jane Hedal-Siegel, Aimee Bench, Jeannie Schultz, Melissa Menta, Rana Komar, Steve Dale, and Bernard Clair.

Everyone at NBC Universal who is involved with the production of the Westminster and National Dog Shows: Jon Miller, Kevin Monaghan, Gordon Beck, Steve Griffith, Joe Garagiola, Mary Carillo, John O'Hurley; and Candy Caciolo and Ann Viklund of Purina.

Monsignor Thomas Modugno of St. Monica's and Father Ray Nobiletti and Linda Woo of Transfiguration Church and School.

My *Angel By My Side* family: Mike and Nancy

Lingenfelter, Dakota, and Ogilvie.

Delta Society, past and present: Mal Schwartz, Dr. Gregg Takashima and the board, Dr. Bill McCulloch, Maureen MacNamara, Lynnette Eastlake, Linda Hines, Jon Eastlake, Sophie Engelhard Craighead, Megan Wolfe, Carol Cullum, and all of the very special Pet Partner teams.

My friends Ben Walker, Gary and Larry Sever, Bob Clampett, Jeff High, Jeff Wohler, and Bob Main; and my sisters and brother Nancy McCormick, Susan Earley, Judy Kaplan, and Terry Frei.

Andrew DePrisco, Allan Reznik, and Amy Deputato at BowTie, and my agent, Steve Sadicario: thanks to all of you for believing in me and what I do and for making this book possible.

And last, but hardly least, the bravest kids in the world: Andrea, Anthony, Jessie, Laura, Dylan, Eden, George, Devin, Millie, Mitch, Uri, Raisa, Alyssa, Deyja, Fitzgerald, and more; their parents and families; Karen, Belinda, and Maria; and the nurses and staff everywhere we visit.

And of course, the Good Lord, for blessing me with all of these wonderful people and dogs in my life. Thank you.

Introduction:
You Have Me

In 2007, the great dog photographer Mary Bloom took a shot of Teigh and me at an outdoor dog show. It was a hot day, and he was sitting on my lap. I didn't see the photo until it ran in *Dog Fancy* magazine a couple of months later. It's a great shot—I love it—and I have named it the "you-really-do-start-to-look-like-your-dog-as-you-get-older" picture.

But the real impact of the picture is that we are both smiling. Yes, my dog is smiling.

My dogs do something to make me smile every day, and I try to reciprocate. Judging from this picture of the two of us, maybe I'm succeeding. People always say that they want to come back in another life as my dog, and I think that being my dog is a pretty good deal for both of us!

This little verse from the brilliant humorist Roy Blount Jr., written underneath a picture of a Standard Poodle reclining in an easy chair, is told from the perspective of the dog and tells you everything about the relationship between most people and their dogs.

∞

You could say I have it pretty good
Here, you could.
But then too, you see,
You have me.

Roy Blount Jr.
I Am Puppy, Hear Me Yap:
The Ages of Dog (2000)

Do you call your dogs "the kids"? Have you ever bought a car because it was the right car for the family dog? Or rented or bought a house because you wanted the space or yard for your dog? Have you ever planned a vacation based on the idea that you wanted the dog to come along? Do you go to sidewalk cafes for dinner so you can take your dog along?

Guilty on all counts, your honor.

We have this great spiritual and emotional connection to our dogs today—they are members of our families, a part of everything that we do.

Gone are the days of getting a dog for functional reasons, to do jobs for us. Today, we have dogs for companionship, not to pull carts or hunt snow leopards or drive our cattle to market. Of course, there are some exceptions, but more Labrador Retrievers join us as family dogs than as hunters. I could go on and on, but why don't you just tune in to the Westminster Kennel Club or the National Dog Show telecast to hear more from me about what the different breeds were originally bred to do?

Dog owners are special. Bringing a dog into your life creates a relationship with responsibilities and obligations. My wife and I coordinate our office hours based on the dogs' schedules. Our lives depend on dog walkers, veterinarians, and pet-supply store hours and deliveries. Our response to every invitation that we receive always depends on the answer to the question "What about the dogs?"

Bringing a dog into your life is also a sign of sharing and self-giving. And I happen to believe that's exactly why so many people and their dogs are getting involved in therapy dog work these days.

I have been truly blessed. I have a wonderful life, thanks to my family, thanks to some great jobs, and thanks to my life in dogs, which includes showing dogs, my work as the voice of the Westminster Kennel Club and the National Dog Show, and my involvement with our wonderful therapy dog charity, Angel On A Leash.

I have had a lot of fun along the way. Dogs have taken me to the White House, to visit with military heroes at Walter Reed Army Medical Center and Fort Sam Houston, for a ride on a float in the Macy's Thanksgiving Day Parade, and to a role on *Sex and the City*. I've been on the *Food Network Challenge* as a judge in a cake-baking contest and have appeared on the *Martha Stewart Show*, the *Ellen DeGeneres Show*, the *Today Show*, *Good Morning America*, and many more, usually accompanied by a dog or bringing a dog-related message.

I met a special man, Mike Lingenfelter, and his amazing service dog, Dakota, and together we wrote a book to tell his story, *The Angel by My Side*. The book won two awards from the Dog Writers Association of America in 2003.

I've met a cardinal and an archbishop and many celebrities because of the dogs. But with apologies to all of them, the biggest celebrity that I've ever been around just may have been the inimitable Westminster Best in Show Beagle, Uno. The real stars in my world have four legs. Because of my own dogs—going to dog shows with them, walking the streets with them, and everything I do with them—I've met some of the most wonderful people, too.

My dogs are Angel On A Leash therapy dogs, and as we proudly say about all of our Angel On A Leash dogs, all therapy dogs are champions. My dogs have delivered me to special places such as Ronald McDonald House

New York, Memorial Sloan-Kettering Cancer Center in New York, the NewYork-Presbyterian Morgan Stanley Children's Hospital, and the Transfiguration Church and School of Manhattan's Chinatown.

I've met lots of special people and courageous warriors of all ages. My dogs are changing people's lives and taking me along, changing my life, too. The stories in this book that have come from our adventures are both heartwarming and heartbreaking, and I have learned so much from all of the experiences that I share. I am honored and humbled to tell these stories. I have been touched by the special people that I've met, thanks to my special dogs, Teigh, Belle, Angel, and Grace.

The Bible tells us that "A faithful friend is the medicine of life and immortality." I thank my faithful friends every day for letting me be the guy on the other end of the leash. They are my heroes for what they teach me—unconditional love, patience, compassion, caring, how to be nonjudgmental, and more. We add to that list every day.

Before you dive into this book, stop right now and hug your dog. In fact, I hope that you will find many other stops along the way where you will be moved to put down this book for a moment and hug your dog again. And again. And again.

Scout has taught me that you don't need to go through life in a hurry. You see so much more when you go slow.

—BERN

CHAPTER 1

Wisdom

Scout, a sweetheart of a black Lab from the end of the block, was out for her usual morning stroll in the neighborhood, slowly accompanying her human on their daily trip to the local bodega for coffee and a newspaper.

Her human is my friend Bern. He's a big-time attorney, but on the street in the early morning hours he's just another dog guy in a hat and T-shirt with a plastic bag, doing his morning routine. Like many of us in our Upper East Side neighborhood here in New York City, he is known more for his dog and consequently is "Scout's dad" to a lot of folks.

Here, if you're out walking your dog (or dogs), you just come to expect that any greeting goes first to the dog—"Hey, Scout!"After that, you might get an acknowledgment, perhaps something less enthusiastic than the greeting that your dog got. And, even though people are quick to know your dog, they might not know your name—you'll often have to settle for a nod and "How ya doin'?"

I used to own two sports bars in Seattle, and our regular customers often took on their identity with us according to what they always ordered: "Bud in a bottle"..."Stoli and tonic"..."bacon cheeseburger"... and so on. Same thing for all of us on East 72nd Street when it came to our dogs: "Poodle guy"..."Dachshund lady"..."Pug man"...

But with those who we see regularly, we do in fact have names for the dogs and their people: Elsie and Judith, Arthur and Norma, Morgan and Ed, Meggie and Karen, Lucy and Nicole, Jack and Jim and Felix, Lady and Maria, Cardozo and David, Butter and Seraphina and Michelle, and many more.

Those of us with dogs will tell you that our dogs define the neighborhood culture and social scene. The dogs are the great equalizers, bringing people together every day. It often starts with the very simple request: "May I pet your dog?" There is no phrase that brings together people any better than that one does. Diplomats should all get dogs and get to work making friends with each other.

Cheri and I joke that we might not know anyone in our neighborhood if we didn't have dogs. Instead, we have a rich collection of friends and acquaintances: doormen, parking attendants, food vendors, street characters, nurses and doctors and other medical professionals heading to work at the nearby hospitals, people with their earbuds in, people in business suits, people in T-shirts, people hauling their children around, people just hanging out.

At the age of thirteen, Scout was slowing down, and her one-block journey each morning was becoming more and more labored. Nonetheless, Bern faithfully and patiently allowed Scout this daily ritual, no doubt knowing how much it must have meant to her to have the time with him. My guess was that for Bern, it wasn't about the coffee—it was a combination of his sense of duty and his love for Scout. It was wonderful to witness this two-way devotion every morning.

When you have a dog, whether or not you are smart enough to realize it, this faithfulness and patience in the daily routine from start to finish is part of the deal. So in spite of the fact that we were watching Scout nearing the end of her life, we could all smile at what we got to see every day. I know that Bern would have done anything for Scout, and Scout would have done anything for Bern. She may not have done it as quickly as she would have in the past, but she would have done it.

One morning, watching Bern head back up the street with Scout, I said to him, "I guess you don't have many early morning appointments at the office these days."

He paused, looked at Scout, and smiled. She kept trudging along, not wanting to slow her momentum. She knew that he would catch up.

"You know," he said, "Scout has taught me that you don't need to go through life in a hurry. You see so much more when you go slow."

Ah, wisdom. Bern's a smart guy; he gets it. But as good an attorney as he might be, I bet he rarely says anything this powerful in any courtroom. I am never surprised by the simple eloquence that dogs inspire from their people.

Scout passed shortly after this, and all of us in the neighborhood mourned the loss of a family member. It doesn't take Bern as long to get to the bodega every morning now, but I'm sure that Scout is still making that trip with him every day. And even better, she left him with a piece of wisdom that may not be taught in law school, or in any school, for that matter.

In my world of dog shows and training, we always worry so much about what we teach our dogs—to stand, to move, to heel, to sit, to behave—and that's a good thing. But as we saw with Scout, what's far more important is what we learn from our dogs.

So pay attention.

I Get It

Dogs are spontaneous. They live in the moment. They react to anything and everything that we say or do. They live, love, celebrate, and mourn with us whenever we give them the chance.

Interact with a dog—pet him, talk to him, feed him a cookie, go for a walk with him—and you feel better. Dog owners have known that intuitively for years; it's a concept that anyone who has a dog understands. It's the dog greeting you at the door, tail wagging at full speed, after you've had a long, tough day at the office. It's the dog sitting next to you on the couch, putting his head on your lap when you need a little something.

It's unconditional love. Your dog doesn't care about appearances or how much money you make or how you talk. He just loves you, and he loves you every waking moment, whether or not you have good shoes.

It's the combination of that spontaneity and the unconditional love that they give us every day that makes dogs so good at therapy work. No expectations, no grudges, no charge for the service. Well, maybe a good scratch *right there ... thank you very much.*

I've been seeing this spontaneity and unconditional love happening with my dogs for a lot of years. In fact, I saw these things before I ever got serious about therapy dogs, but I just never really put it all together.

And here is how we know that it works: when a dog walks into the room, the energy changes.

The dog doesn't need to be a high-profile show dog like Westminster Best in Show winners Uno, Rufus, or James, or a TV star like Lassie or *Frasier*'s Eddie. And the place doesn't need to be a hospital or a nursing home. Any dog can make this happen, and it can happen anywhere. Sure, we see wonderful pictures of dogs visiting children, spending time with seniors, or comforting wounded military members in health care facilities. But it can happen for your elderly neighbor who lives alone, for someone you meet walking down the street, or right in your own living room just for you.

Maybe it's the anticipation of that spontaneity or that unconditional love. Look! It's a dog! Look at that haircut, look how excited he is to be here, look at his tail ... wow! I want to pet him!

Suddenly, someone is thinking about something other than his or her challenges or pain or a grim outlook or the next treatment. Right now, for this moment, it's not about the person, it's about the dog.

Next, maybe it manifests itself in a smile—a smile from someone who hasn't had much to smile about. I can't tell you how often a parent has said to me as his or her child is petting or hugging or watching my dog: "That's the first time she's smiled this week."

Maybe it's a laugh or a few words or a step out of a stroller or wheelchair. Maybe it's a lucid moment for someone, a look back in time at his or her own dog. It could be any or all of those things.

Is it magic? Perhaps. Are we changing people's lives? Yes, we are. Maybe only for the moment, but yes, we are.

• • • • • •

And speaking of changing people's lives, here's how it happened to me. When two spontaneous, unconditional-loving, energy-changing, orange-and-white dogs charged into my world in 1999 and brought their blonde Jersey girl owner with them, my life changed.

The dogs' names were Teigh and Belle. They were happy, enthusiastic, energetic Brittanys who loved everyone they met. I didn't know it at the time and would have laughed if anyone had said it to me, but they were going to teach me about life.

The girl's name was Cherilyn, and she was a graduate student at Seattle University pursuing her master's degree in theology. Her thesis was going to be on animal-assisted therapy. She had heard me mention therapy dogs on the Westminster telecast and asked a mutual friend to introduce us so we could talk about therapy dogs. She had just started visiting Seattle's Swedish Medical Center with Teigh, and she was competing with Belle at dog shows.

I was smitten by all three of them, and soon we were together. Cheri continued to pursue her degree, and

I often served as the handler for Teigh and Belle, her "demo dogs," in her presentations. I learned a lot from her as she worked her way through academia. Actually, I learned a lot about myself, as well—that was the life-changing part of the deal.

While all of this was going on, I still had my own public relations business in Seattle, and one of my clients was Delta Society, the world's leading organization for therapy dogs. A great client, a nice fit, and Cheri was a big help in handling the production of their Beyond Limits Awards, which were presented annually to the therapy dog and service dog teams of the year.

I went with Cheri a few times on her therapy visits with Teigh, and I helped her with presentations at Seattle University and Providence Hospital. I thought I would try to become trained and registered with Belle as a therapy dog team as a way to learn about animal-assisted therapy. I thought that I could support Cheri and her work if I was involved myself, and I thought that we could do good things for people in need. But, admittedly, while helping people in need was a positive thing, at the outset my intent was mostly to learn about the work that my client did and to be supportive of my wife and her studies—what was to become her life's work. Belle and I went through the training class and passed.

I did some visiting with Cheri at some of the places she had been working, but after watching her in action and hearing some of her stories about her other experiences, I thought I should see what it was like on my own with Belle. The first visit that Belle and I did was to an extended care facility in north Seattle. Visits to extended care facilities (they used to be called nursing homes) can be somewhat uncomplicated, as the people there are relatively quiet and the situation is not too stressful for the dog or the handler. I thought this would be the perfect maiden voyage for us.

The administrator greeted me, and I introduced him to Belle. She gave him the standard Brittany greeting: the butt wiggle, the lean-in, and the wagging tail. He loved her. Of course. I was certain that she would get the same reaction from the people we were about to visit, and I was anxious to get started.

The administrator walked us down the hall. He told me that he was bringing me first to Richard, a long-term care patient who had a photo in his room of himself with a Brittany. However, Richard was battling the early stages of dementia, the administrator told me, and I shouldn't expect too much from him. Richard also believed that his family had simply dumped him in the facility to live out his days. "He's not happy to be here," said the administrator. "He's rarely spoken and rarely smiled since he arrived here some three months ago."

With that information, Belle and I entered Richard's room. I was a little anxious and was hoping for just about any reaction from him—a smile, maybe a few words. We walked in, Belle tugging me along with her tail wagging and her body twisting in that Brittany kind of way. She apparently had not heard anything that the administrator had told me, and she was ready to make a new friend.

Instantly, we got the smile—and then some. Richard's smile lit up the room, his face beaming, tears forming in his eyes. All at once, he became animated and vocal.

"Come here, you knucklehead," he called to Belle, slapping his thigh. She jumped on his lap and he hugged her as the administrator's eyes widened at this first show of emotion. I watched without speaking, but I was thinking, *Geez, we're already breaking the rules by letting her jump on his lap.*

I decided, given what I had been told coming in, that this was a rule that could be broken for Richard. The interaction was exciting to watch, actually.

By the way he was talking to her, I quickly realized that Richard thought Belle was his dog. He confirmed that when he said to me, "Son, will you take care of her after I die?" When his tears started flowing, so did mine.

Belle could feel what was happening, and she was loving it. Here she was—the dog who runs through my house at about 40 miles an hour, the dog who chases pigeons, squirrels, and her brother throughout our urban neighborhood, now just patiently resting her head on Richard's lap—looking him right in those tear-filled eyes.

When it was time to move on, Richard gave Belle a big hug, some more pets, and said good-bye. He was smiling. He was happy. Maybe just for that moment, but that's the moment we have, the moment we want, and the moment we contribute to.

We wandered through the facility and had a couple more visits. Belle stuck her face onto the bed of another man, who was bedridden but smiling. She sat on a chair and went eye-to-eye with a woman who produced a smile that she apparently had never given in this place before. She lay on a bed next to another woman who couldn't talk.

On the drive home, I realized that now I got it. Richard and those other people we had visited—we had made their day. Had we changed their lives? Well, at least for that day, we certainly had.

· · · · · ·

Eventually, I passed the evaluation with Teigh, and Cheri passed with Belle. I was ready to set out on my own with Teigh and Belle. I had lost a few friends from the dog show world to AIDS in the past ten years, so I thought I would volunteer in their memory at Bailey-Boushay House in Seattle, an AIDS hospice.

I understood the basics about hospices: that they are administering palliative care, and the idea is that they are helping people deal with the end of their lives. I really hadn't been around a lot of death, and while I wasn't reluctant to do what I could to help, it was going to be a new experience for me.

I came away from the volunteer orientation believing that Bailey-Boushay was good at this, but I was anxious to see the reality versus the classroom. To me, death was always sad; here, they were trying to show that passing peacefully could perhaps ease some of that sadness.

On our first day, Teigh and I showed up and went right to the nurses' station. It seemed a little quiet, almost grim, but this came as no surprise. As soon as one of the nurses saw Teigh, she broke into a big smile, dropped to her knees, and started talking to him.

"Hey buddy, how are you?" Teigh lay down and rolled over onto his back, ready to make some new friends. "What's your name?"

"He's Teigh, and I'm David," I said. "This is our first visit here."

"Well, Teigh and David, we are so glad that you are here," she said. I could feel that her remark was more than just some platitude. Another nurse joined in with the stomach rubs while several others watched and smiled, stopping what they were doing at the moment. We would always be greeted in this fashion at B-B. After a few visits, I could understand why.

People were dying there every day. I would come back every Tuesday and be unable to find one or two people that I had seen the week before. Sometimes it was expected, sometimes not. I am sure that the people who worked with this every day could find it a little grim, even if helping the dying was their life's work. So I came to realize that here, visiting the staff was just as important as—maybe even more so than—visiting the patients. They, too, needed some revitalization, something to make them smile or just help them move on after losing a patient.

After working our way through the staff, we would have quite a variety of patients waiting for us. They all had different stories, and many of them wanted to share those stories with us, perhaps in kind of a cleansing process as they were preparing to die.

Their stories weren't what mattered to Teigh or to me. We were there to get some smiles and some pets for Teigh, whether from a well-to-do gay man, a tough street person, or a woman dying of cancer. Teigh would crawl into bed with some of them, sit in a chair next to the bed with others, or just hang quietly in my arms. Already I found myself wanting to be just like Teigh, with his measured enthusiasm and his ability to draw out some difficult smiles.

Cheri soon finished her master's degree and was ready for her residency at Swedish. About that time, the American Kennel Club (AKC) asked if I would do some work for them as a public relations consultant and public spokesperson. The AKC was headquartered in New York City but told me that I could do the job from Seattle. We made a trip to New York and, while we were there, Cheri was offered a residency at NewYork-Presbyterian/Weill Cornell Medical Center. We decided that we would move to New York.

We were sad to leave Seattle but excited about the professional opportunities in New York. And out in New Jersey, Emily, my mother-in-law, was happy to get her daughter back home.

After a two-year residency at NewYork-Presbyterian Hospital/Weill Cornell, Cheri spent a year as the chaplain and director of pastoral care at Terence Cardinal Cooke Health Care Center in New York. Then, Ronald McDonald House asked her to be its Catholic chaplain and director of family support. That turned out to be a life-changing offer for both of us. Ronald McDonald House is a home-away-from-home for families who would come to New York from all over the world. Here, they hoped to find answers for their children who were fighting battles with cancer and being treated at New York hospitals such as Memorial Sloan-Kettering, New-York-Presbyterian, and New York University.

Meanwhile, the Westminster Kennel Club asked me to come and work for them. I had done their TV commentary on USA Network since 1990, so we were not strangers. They created a full-time position for me as director of communications, and I moved a few blocks south on Madison Avenue from the AKC to Westminster in 2003.

The following year, I suggested that Westminster consider creating and supporting a charitable activity that combined dogs with children—something to bring the club into a new part of the New York City community. We were very active in a number of dog-related charities, but as the kennel club of New York, we could do more. I suggested a therapy dog program at the NewYork-Presbyterian Morgan Stanley Children's Hospital, something that would bring us into the area of helping humans. I also suggested the name "Angel On A Leash," and we all agreed that it was a perfect description. So we were off and running, soon adding Ronald McDonald House New York and Providence Medical Center in Portland, Oregon, as Angel facilities.

• • • • • •

Anyone who shares his or her life with a dog understands intuitively the magic that dogs bring into our lives. I know what my dogs do for me, and I know what they do for others—no one needs to tell me why or how. Lately, though, science is catching up to our intuition. We are learning the physiology behind it all. Studies have shown that when you interact with a dog, whether it's petting a dog or just looking at a dog and smiling, it increases the flow of endorphins, the "good" hormones, and that makes you feel better. When you feel better, your blood pressure goes down and your heart rate goes down.

We call it the therapeutic touch. There are more and

more studies being published every day that back this up. Here are some, as reported by Delta Society:

- A 2005 study by the American Heart Association showed that heart patients visited by therapy dogs experienced a reduction in stress levels.
- A 2004 study by Rebecca Johnson, PhD, RN, of the University of Missouri-Columbia Center for the Study of Animal Wellness, showed that when a human pets a dog, it launches a release of hormones such as beta-endorphin, prolactin, dopamine, and oxytocin, all associated with good health. This was the first time that a therapeutic relationship between animals and humans had been scientifically measured.
- An earlier study at the State University of New York at Buffalo by Dr. Karen Allen evaluated forty-eight stock-brokers who were taking medication for hypertension. The study found that the brokers who were given a pet saw their stress levels drop significantly, and half of them were able to go off their medication.
- Studies reported in the *American Journal of Cardiology* in 2003 found that pet owners have shorter hospital stays, make fewer doctor visits, and take less medication for high blood pressure and cholesterol that those who do not own pets.
- The Chimo Project in Alberta, Canada, compared animal-assisted therapy with traditional therapy for patients in treatment for depression and anxiety in a twenty-seven-month project that began in 2001. The patients who met with therapists who used dogs in their sessions looked forward to therapy more, felt more comfortable talking to the therapists, and felt

that they performed better at home and school than patients receiving traditional therapy. Patients who had pets were less depressed or anxious at the outset and showed lower scores on the depression severity scale after therapy than those who did not own pets.

But I found that it still is more than science and physiology. It's spirituality, too. Dogs are faithful friends, gifts from whomever or wherever you believe they come from. They are blessings, and we give thanks for our blessings by sharing them with others.

· · · · · ·

About the time that Cheri came into my life and brought me Teigh and Belle, I read *Tuesdays with Morrie*, the great book by Mitch Albom. Mitch was a sportswriter from Detroit who rediscovered one of his college professors, Morrie, who was in the last months of his life. The book tells of a series of visits between the two men in which Morrie shares his life lessons.

Morrie talked about devoting yourself to loving others, devoting yourself to the community around you, and devoting yourself to creating something that gives you purpose and meaning. With all of that, Morrie said that you should choose to live a life that matters, offering to others what you have to give—specifically love and compassion. I never got to meet Morrie, but I did read the book. And just as good, I had Teigh and Belle to teach me about unconditional love. They helped me choose what I believe to be a life that matters. Teigh and Belle changed my life.

Their spontaneity and total honesty might just be what makes dogs so good at therapy work. Many of the patients we visit have to live their lives in the moment because, sadly, that's all that they have. But that's perfect for the dogs because they live their lives in the moment, too. And it's perfect for our visits because we visit in the moment.

Perfect.

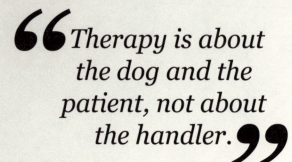 *Therapy is about the dog and the patient, not about the handler.*

Stay Out of Their Way

I believe that good therapy dogs are born, not made. It is mostly a personality and temperament thing. They don't have to be a particular breed; a therapy dog can be any breed or a mixed breed. While some breeds are inherently better at it than others, it is still an individual thing that is also dependent on the handler.

Therapy dogs need to have positive, happy, accepting personalities. Sure, they need some basic obedience training, but more important, they have to be able to tolerate and withstand, with help from their handlers, loud noises and awkward situations. They have to enjoy attention and being around people, but not necessarily all people. Some therapy dogs enjoy rambunctious kids, while some of them prefer more sedate seniors. Some of them love lying quietly with patients on their beds, and some of them need to chase a ball and roll over to have their stomachs rubbed.

The human half of the therapy dog team—and it is important to remember that it is a team—can mess things up. It can come from trying too hard, from being too protective, or from pushing a dog into a situation that he doesn't like. Or it can just be because the person doesn't get it. Therapy is about the dog and the patient, not about the handler. In that sense, it's very similar to what I always say about handlers in the dog show ring—the best handlers are almost invisible. That doesn't mean that they don't have a presence and an important role, but the best therapy dog handlers are guiding, not leading, and protecting, not pushing.

Angel On A Leash was a subject for a piece on the *Today Show* a couple of years ago. It was a wonderful story that was reported by Jill Rappaport, featuring interviews and video from Morgan Stanley Children's Hospital and from Ronald McDonald House, and closing with Teigh, Belle, and me in the studio.

Host Meredith Vieira asked me, "David, when you're out there doing your thing with your dogs, what is going through your mind? What's the most important thing that you are thinking about?"

That was an easy answer.

"Just stay out of their way," I said.

• • • • • •

I get a lot of people who come up to me and say something like, "My dog will make a great therapy dog; she's ready to go right now. You've seen her out here in the neighborhood. Why do we have to go through the training class?"

I tell them that the training is almost more for the people than the dogs (and occasionally I think, *especially you*). Sometimes I tell them that with a little wink, and sometimes I just send a little thought to the dog: "Good luck with your human."

There are a number of therapy dog organizations out there that train, evaluate, and register therapy dogs. My personal favorite is Delta Society of Bellevue, Washington, which is our preference and recommendation for all of our Angel On A Leash facilities. I am a past board member and public relations consultant for Delta and have been familiar with their work for a long time, dating back to my days in Seattle.

Delta Society was formed in 1977 by a number of visionaries from the human and veterinary health fields. Psychiatrist Dr. Michael McCulloch and veterinarians Dr. Leo Bustad and Dr. Bill McCulloch were the leaders of a group of professionals who had seen the human-animal bond providing positive effects on their clients and patients.

Delta grew into an international organization emphasizing animal-assisted activities and animal-assisted therapy. From Delta's website (www.deltasociety.org):

> Animal-assisted activities (AAA) are basically the casual "meet and greet" activities that involve pets visiting people. The same activity can be repeated with many people, unlike a therapy program that is tailored to a particular person or medical condition.
>
> Animal-assisted therapy (AAT) is a goal-directed intervention in which an animal that meets specific criteria is an integral part of the treatment process. AAT is directed and/or delivered by a health/human service professional with special-

ized expertise, and within the scope of practice of his/her profession. AAT is designed to promote improvement in human physical, social, emotional, and/or cognitive functioning.

Today, Delta Society has more than 10,000 registered Pet Partner teams (dog and handler) across the country, along with a nationwide network of evaluators and instructors. The heart and soul of the Pet Partner program is the twenty-two-point evaluation process for potential teams. Each dog also must undergo a thorough veterinary health screening before the team can be registered.

Unlike most other therapy dog registries, Delta Society requires Pet Partner teams to be reevaluated every two years. This is important for many reasons. Sometimes dogs change after passing the initial evaluation. For example, maybe a dog had a bad experience on a visit or he just doesn't like therapy work anymore. Maybe his body has changed, and he now is experiencing new pain issues. Perhaps a dog has developed some tender spots due to arthritis and aging or perhaps from an injury. What happens if a patient accidentally touches the wrong spot, and the dog cries out in pain or turns and nips someone? Is that the dog's fault? I think it's the fault of the handler either for not knowing his or her dog well enough to be aware of the problem or for knowing about it and putting the dog in an untenable situation anyway.

Delta's requirements for timely (at least twice a year) veterinary exams and evaluations by certified instructors/evaluators can head off potentially troublesome (or dangerous) situations. These evaluations, health screenings, and registration renewals every two years

make me a big fan. So does the $1,000,000 liability in-
surance coverage of its teams. That should also make
any facility a big fan.

Unfortunately, not all therapy dog organizations
are alike.

I spoke to a person who runs a therapy dog training
organization, which will remain nameless. I asked her if
her group had liability insurance on its teams. She said,
"No, they don't need it. They are trained so well that they
will never have a problem."

I was stunned. I think that I am a good driver, but
I would never get behind the wheel without insurance.
We all believe that our dogs will never create or be a
problem, but what if?

I had another issue with the same organization. When
teams "graduated" from the program, they were given
vests that said "service dog" on them and were told that
they could now take their dogs on airplanes, into public
places such as restaurants, and the like. Now we're talking criminal activity, and this leads me into a rant that I
have to recite way too often.

Therapy dogs are not service dogs. There is a significant difference. Because of this difference, therapy dogs
do not get the same kind of access, guaranteed by federal law, as service dogs.

According to Delta Society, a service dog is "any dog
individually trained to do work or perform tasks for the
benefit of a person with a disability."

A disability is defined on the Delta Society website
as "any physical or mental condition which substan-
tially limits a major life activity such as caring for one's
self, performing manual tasks, walking, seeing, hearing,

speaking, breathing, learning, and working." Many people have hidden disabilities (e.g., epilepsy, heart disease, hearing problems), and that complicates compliance and enforcement issues.

Complicating things further, the law does not require a person to show any proof that the dog is a service dog; does not require that the dog wear any special tag, equipment, or vest; and does not require the handler to divulge any details about his or her disability. However, airlines recently have been given the right to require some kind of documentation for certain service dog requests.

Service dogs are guaranteed access to any place that their people go, including restaurants, taxis, airplanes, trains, stores, and theaters. This is a federal law covered by the Americans with Disabilities Act of 1990.

I learned a little about service dogs when I cowrote *The Angel by My Side* (www.angelbymyside.com) with Mike Lingenfelter in 2002 (see chapter 15). It was the wonderful story of Mike and his heroic service dog, Dakota. We were proud that the book won two awards from the Dog Writers Association of America that year, but prouder still of being able to tell the story.

Mike is my "go-to guy" for issues having to do with service dogs. Dakota alerted on Mike when Mike was about to have a heart attack (unstable angina). Dakota could sense Mike's oncoming attacks before Mike could, and that gave Mike the chance to take his medication a little earlier and head off the worst of it.

Mike looked pretty normal (still does), so he spent a lot of time fighting accessibility battles with restaurants and other places when he came in with Dakota. Relating those stories in our book taught me about the challenges that people with service dogs have to face every day, and I found myself a firsthand observer of some of them.

Mike is one of those people with a service dog who also uses his dog as a therapy dog to help others. This happened because Dakota came to him as a therapy dog and by chance eventually also became his service dog. This can be difficult for the dog, because a service dog needs to be totally devoted to taking care of his human and to ignore the people around them, while in therapy dog work, a dog needs to interact with people other than his handler/human partner. It takes a special dog to be able to do both jobs well.

However, therapy dogs are usually not service dogs and, as I mentioned, do not have the same rights of access as service dogs. Therapy dogs are part of a human/dog team and are used primarily in health care facilities to promote human health and well-being.

Unfortunately, the laws guaranteeing accessibility for service dogs are abused by dog owners who want their dogs to come with them everywhere for various reasons (including travel). These people are easy to recognize. I saw someone in Denver International Airport with a lovely Golden Retriever. The dog did not have a vest (remember, service dogs do not need one) and, admittedly, could very well have been a service dog. I watched the dog's owner drag the dog onto an escalator, something that frightened (and endangered) the dog, in spite of the fact that there was an elevator within eyesight of this escalator. The "scam alert" bell went off in my mind. Whether you have a service dog, a therapy dog, or a pet, you do not take a dog onto an escalator unless you are holding him in your arms. I knew that if the owner didn't already know this, he didn't take his dog very many places, which made me think that perhaps this wasn't a service dog who should be going everywhere with his human.

Another red flag was that this poor dog was frightened of the escalator, understandably enough, but his clueless handler put the dog in danger anyway. A trained service dog is unflappable.

Therapy dogs do wonderful things for people in need, but people who use the status of therapy dog certification to abuse accessibility issues are jeopardizing the rights of legitimate service dogs, and, more critically, they are making the lives of the human partners of service dogs much more difficult than they already are. I know a lot of people who depend on their service dogs every waking moment. They already have to fight battles every day over accessibility for their life-saving, four-legged partners.

People who abuse therapy dog certification in this manner had better hope that they don't run into me. Or Mike. But I digress.

My original point when I began is that not all therapy dog organizations are alike. There are some, unfortunately, that may as well just ask you to send in three dog-food labels and a few bucks in exchange for your therapy dog registration. There are a few organizations out there that exist only on a website and will be happy to send you a certificate in exchange for something (usually money). You need to know that it is not that simple.

If a therapy dog organization that you are researching does not make you work at your certification, does not require your dog to be checked by a veterinarian, does not evaluate and reevaluate you and your dog, and does not provide some type of continuing contact, then avoid that organization. You won't be properly prepared, and neither will your dog, and someone could end up getting hurt. Your dog could get hurt.

If a working therapy dog causes a problem in a health care facility because the dog or handler is improperly trained, unprepared, or unhealthy, or if the dog is not properly insured or not appropriate for visiting, then all of us involved in therapy work are going to pay for it, no matter what with which organization we are registered.

If you want to become part of a therapy dog team, please do something for me, for the facilities that our teams visit, for the people who volunteer, for the people who benefit from our visits, and for the medical professionals who believe in us and support our work—do us all a favor. And do yourself a favor. Maintain and protect the integrity of the work by dealing with therapy dog organizations that do it right, as described above.

For Angel On A Leash facilities, we ask that our teams be registered through Delta Society. That way, we know how they have been trained and evaluated, that they are being provided with $1,000,000 in liability insurance coverage by their registering organization, that their health status is continuously monitored, and that they are subject to timely reevaluations. Recognizing that you may face geographic challenges in finding an organization, you should know that there may be other registering bodies that do this, too, but keep these key points in mind as you move forward with your dog.

· · · · · ·

While the American Kennel Club does not certify therapy dogs, it now works with over fifty-five organizations that register therapy dogs, including Bright and Beautiful Therapy Dogs, Delta Society Pet Partners Program, Love on a Leash, Therapy Dogs Incorporated (TD Inc.), and Therapy Dogs International (TDI), to recognize the great work that dogs do in this area. In addition to the AKC's recognition of one outstanding therapy dog as part of its annual AKC Humane Fund Awards for Canine Excellence (ACE), in 2011 the club began offering the AKC Therapy Dog title (THD). The criteria for the title require that a registered therapy dog be either registered or listed with the AKC (this includes purebred and mixed-breed dogs) and perform no fewer than fifty community service visits. For more information, visit www.akc.org/akctherapydog.

Just Whistle if You Need Me

When I first moved to New York, my friend Karen LeFrak suggested that I bring my dogs to join her and her Standard Poodles, Jewel and Diamond, in visiting at Mount Sinai Medical Center, and we jumped right in. When I first started there, we could only visit patients in the recreational therapy room; no in-room visits were allowed. The physical therapists would bring the patients to us, and that could create some special moments.

One night, Teigh and I had just completed a quiet visit with a patient. I looked across the room and saw two boys, maybe in their late teens, sitting in high-backed wheelchairs. In front of them were a man and a woman, each of them feeding one of the boys. I guessed that the boys were brothers and that the man and woman were their parents. They seemed a little grim, so I also surmised that the boys were quadriplegic. I had no way of knowing, but perhaps the best guess was that they had been in some kind of an auto accident.

Teigh looked over at them and apparently caught the eye of one of the boys. The boy whistled. Teigh's ears went up, and he stood and started to wag his tail. The mother looked at me and smiled. I asked, "Can we come over and visit?" Mom looked to Dad, and I surmised a little more—that they and may not speak English. She said something to him in Spanish, and he looked at us and waved us over.

We walked across the room, and I said to the group, "Hi, my name is David, and this is Teigh, my therapy dog." I got a smiling, wordless response. OK, so they don't speak English. Try again. "Hola, soy David y este es mi perro, Teigh." Smiles from all. *Please no more Spanish*, I thought. *That's all I got.*

The father pointed: "Miguel ... Juanito." I pointed to him and his wife: "Padre y madre?" "Si."

The boys were smiling but not too active, as one might imagine. Teigh went to the whistler—Miguel—first, and sat down in front of him, looking up at him. Miguel whistled again, and it became very evident to me that he couldn't move his arms. Teigh tilted his head from side to side and stood up. One more whistle. Teigh lay down and rolled over. Laughter all around.

I was thrilled with this, and he had done it without any prompting from me. *Good boy, Teigh.* He stood there, wagging his little stub of a tail, soaking up the excitement. He found a scrap of food on the floor, probably something that had fallen off the tray. I'm not really supposed to encourage him to do that, but I saw that it was a piece of bread, so I pretended not to notice that he had found some contraband.

Next, I directed Teigh over in front of the other boy.

Juanito was still smiling, but apparently he couldn't whistle like his brother. That was OK, because what he could do was move his right arm. He slid his arm over to the side and dropped it off the tray so that his hand landed palm open and facing Teigh.

Teigh, God love him, ran right over there and high-fived him, slapping his paw into Juanito's open palm. Madre was crying; Padre was fighting back the tears; the boys were laughing it up. I knew that they hadn't had a moment like this for a while. Teigh found another scrap of food on the floor and seemed to know that it was put there for him.

Madre and Padre reached down and petted Teigh in a most loving way; I know that they were saying thanks for the moment. Teigh's exit move, this time with a little direction from the guy on the other end of his leash, was another rollover. Lots of smiles and wide eyes.

It was a great walk home for us that night.

· · · · · ·

Mount Sinai was several blocks from our apartment, and most nights I would want to take a cab so that Teigh or Belle wouldn't get too dirty walking there. It often could be tough to get a cab to stop for a dog, as the law says that cab drivers have to pick up a service dog, but picking up any other dog is up to them. So there were some things that I would do to help get us a cab.

Most of the time, I would set out for the hospital and just hide the dog behind a garbage can or a mailbox while I flagged down the cab. I would have to be quick enough so that the driver couldn't just drive off upon seeing the dog (which some occasionally did), tossing the dog in the back and then jumping in. I sometimes would have the dogs wearing their therapy vests in the hope that it would let the cab driver know that these were clean, special dogs. That didn't always help, and I usually did not have them in their vests for visits anyway. In any case, finding a cab was often a challenge, and I would sometimes find myself either arguing with drivers who had stopped or shouting something as they drove off.

Once we were in the cab, I would do whatever I could to help future considerations. To begin, the dog would ride on the floor in the back seat, something that I would happily point out. I would also tell drivers that we were going to the hospital to visit people in need, and that the dog had just had a bath. Sometimes that struck a chord with the drivers, sometimes not. In any case, I would always tip a little extra and be sure to thank the drivers for taking the dog.

Are these drivers going to pick up the next dog that they see? Maybe not—but then again, maybe.

One night, a driver picked up Belle and me for the trip to Mount Sinai.

"Hey, thanks for taking the dog," I said as I put her on the floor and told him where we were going.

"Dogs are better than a lot of my passengers," he said. We laughed together. "She looks very nice."

"Thank you from us both," I said, "She just had a bath. I'm glad someone appreciates my hard work. She's a therapy dog on her way to the hospital to visit patients."

"They let her in the hospital?"

(One of the great things about New York City—especially with cab drivers—is the great range of cultures. For many of them, who come from countries and cultures in which dogs are afterthoughts at best and pariahs at worst, having a dog in a hospital is unimaginable. This is something else that makes it difficult to get a cab.)

Opportunity!

Here came the closer in me: "Yes, just petting the dog and talking to her makes people feel better. The people love it, the dog loves it, and I love it, too."

"Very nice," he said as we pulled up to the hospital.

The fare was five dollars, and I pushed a ten-dollar bill over the seat toward him.

He pushed it back. "This is on me. I think it's wonderful what you do."

• • • • • •

A few weeks later, Teigh and I were in the therapy room, getting ready for another night of visiting. The therapy dog program supervisor came into the room and walked over to us.

"I have a special assignment for you tonight," she said. "Follow me." She led Teigh and me over to the door.

"We are going to walk out of this room together," she began. "When we get into the hall, I am going to turn left and you are going to turn right and go down to room 214 and visit with the patient in that room. I am to know nothing about this," she said.

This sounded like the opening scene in *Mission: Impossible*. I was waiting for her to say, "I will disavow any knowledge of your operation."

The reason for this surreptitious approach was because we were still not allowed to visit patients in their rooms. The supervisor told me that the elderly patient in room 214 was a quadriplegic woman who was hurt when she had fallen off a horse recently. The nurses wanted her to see Teigh, but she couldn't get out of bed. I guess I should have felt honored, but I didn't want to jeopardize the entire program by breaking this basic rule.

The supervisor could see what I was thinking. "Don't worry; this is going to work. Just do it." Well, she was the boss.

Two nurses who I recognized were waiting for us at the end of the hall with sly smiles on their faces, indicating to me that they were indeed in on the plan. I picked up Teigh in my arms so the patient would see him right away, and we followed one of the nurses into the room.

"Carolyn, this is David with his dog, Teigh," she introduced us. "We all thought that you would want to have a visit from them."

"Well, I certainly do," she said with a large smile. She was delightful and in good spirits, but bound to the bed as a quadriplegic. I was trying to figure out how to get Teigh to her. I turned to the nurse and asked, "Can I put him in bed with her?"

"I don't know why not," she said.

"Get me a sheet, please, and we'll make this happen."

I threw the sheet over the bed. "Carolyn, we are going to be careful here. Do you have any tubes or sutures?"

"No, I don't think there's anything here that you have to worry about."

So, very carefully, I lifted Teigh onto the bed, placing him on his back, along her side. It's always a bit magical that Teigh doesn't feel like he weighs his 35 pounds when I am lifting him up to a patient.

I took Carolyn's left arm. "Can I move your arm?" I was asking both her and the nurse. Yes from both of them.

I lifted Teigh's head and wrapped Carolyn's arm around him carefully, because it occurred to me that she wouldn't feel it if it was causing a problem. The nurse pushed a chair underneath me at the bedside, and I sat down, holding on to Teigh and Carolyn.

"Are you OK?" I asked.

"I'm just fine," she said. "I'm so glad that you could come."

"Well, we are all making a little history at the hospital tonight. I'm glad it's with you." I said, winking at the nurse. In keeping with the *Mission: Impossible* theme, I was imagining someone standing watch out in the hall.

I asked Carolyn if she had a dog.

"Sure, we have a couple of them at the farm," she said, and that began a delightful conversation about her dogs, her farm, and her horses.

I tested her every once in a while. "Are you comfortable?" I'd ask. "I'm fine, Teigh's fine. It's great to have him up here with me."

We were probably in there for about fifteen or twenty minutes. I never did look over my shoulder; I was more worried about Teigh and his new friend. When it was time to leave, I took Teigh down and pulled the cover sheet off the bed.

"That was a good visit, Carolyn," I said. "It's easy to tell that you're a dog person; you were great with him."

"He was so gentle. I think I was able to feel him a bit."

Well, that would make our night. I wanted to believe it, too. And if Teigh got her to think like that, maybe it could be a little step on the road to recovery of some kind.

• • • • • •

These days, you can't just walk into a health care facility and volunteer. You must undergo extensive orientations, background checks, and health tests. The same goes for the dogs...well, the health tests anyway.

If anyone had done a background check on Teigh and Belle, it would have been discovered that they in fact had once been busted for running loose in Carl Schurz Park on Manhattan's Upper East Side. In all fairness, I contributed to their delinquency.

Many New York City parks have dog runs, of course, and Carl Schurz has two of them—one for large dogs (over 25 pounds) and another for small dogs (under 25 pounds). Brittanys just don't fit in either category. They are just over 30 pounds, but they are a little soft to be running around with Labs and Rottweilers and the other big guys. At the same time, they are too active and a bit too large to be hanging out with the little guys.

Coming from Seattle, we—the dogs and us—were a little spoiled. There, it was relatively easy to find places to turn the dogs loose and let them run to their hearts' content. In New York City, I had to work a little harder. We would head over to Carl Schurz (the park where the mayor's residence, Gracie Mansion, sits) in the early morning hours and turn Teigh and Belle loose when it looked like the coast was clear—no kids, no picnickers, no other dogs. They would chase squirrels in front of the mansion for about ten minutes, tops, and then we would quickly gather up and head for home. Occasionally, a park worker would say something mean to them or to me, but most of the time we didn't cause any issues.

One morning, we were running later than I liked, and there was a little more activity in the park than at our normal time, so I took the dogs down to the basketball/hockey court, which was empty, and turned them loose. Suddenly, it was like a scene out of whatever television cop show you watch. Three official-looking park vehicles pulled up and slammed on their brakes, and people in uniform jumped out and headed right to me. I called the dogs back to me, but I didn't make any sudden moves.

Busted. I pleaded nolo contendere (no contest), accepted the ticket, and went on my way. The fine was $100. I figured that the per-outing cost, factoring in the times we hadn't been caught, was $10. I guess this wasn't documented in any of our permanent records, and we were cleared for volunteer visits.

· · · · · ·

Eventually, therapy dogs were visiting patients' rooms at Mount Sinai with everyone's blessing. It was great because a lot of patients couldn't get up and get to the therapy room, and we didn't want to leave anyone out.

Belle was my partner one night when we visited Alice, who was in the hospital because she had suffered a stroke. She was coherent and in good spirits when we popped in, but she didn't have total control over her body.

I put Belle on the bed with her. Alice's fingers were curled tightly, and it was difficult for her to move her arm, but she still very slowly got her hands on Belle. She was trying to pet her, but she was having a difficult time. Her petting was in the form of small blows to Belle's head—nothing damaging, just more like rough play.

"Oh, I'm trying ... I just don't have control. Maybe you should just take her down."

"No, she's staying right there," I said, winking at Belle, who was looking at me quizzically. "How about if you try to pet her on the back of her neck instead?" I repositioned Alice's hand and arm.

"I don't want to hurt her."

"We won't let that happen," I assured her. I didn't want to cause Alice any anxiety over the fact that she had lost some control of her hand, as this was probably something new to her from the stroke. "We'll find a way to make it work. Belle gets this kinds of petting from kids sometimes, so she's used to it."

I don't know if Belle understood what I had said, but I got a look from her that told me that she wasn't thrilled. "Belle, you're a good girl," I told her. "Alice loves you."

I put my hands on Alice's hand and helped her pet Belle. After a few minutes, both Alice and Belle were less stressed.

We chatted a bit, and Alice told me that she had a dog at home. "Good! We'll keep practicing here so you'll be ready for your own dog when you get back home."

We didn't stay with Alice too long because I didn't want to push Belle. But Alice got a little better through the course of the visit, and I hoped that she would be prepared to deal with her own dog when she got home. Her own dog was going to have to take over the therapy work that Belle had begun.

This Is Why

In 2007, the world-famous Memorial Sloan-Kettering (MSK) Cancer Center in New York City decided that it would allow therapy dogs to visit certain parts of the hospital for the first time in its history. It had always puzzled me that the world-class leader didn't already have a program. Right across the street, at NewYork-Presbyterian Hospital/Weill Cornell, there was a therapy dog program in place. And while I was never privy to any of the process behind finally creating a program at MSK, I knew that the great M.D. Anderson (MDA) Cancer Center in Houston had a thriving therapy dog program. MSK and MDA were always mentioned in the same breath as the international leaders in the field of cancer treatment. They battled in the *U.S. News & World Report* rankings every year for the top spot among cancer hospitals. Shortly after MDA took the top spot away from MSK one year, MSK decided that it should offer a therapy dog program for patients and their families.

Coincidence? Form your own opinion. I have mine.

However it got there, MSK approved a six-month pilot program that would bring therapy dog teams to the tenth floor, Women's Health. The goal, on our side anyway, was to eventually expand the program to other floors if all went well.

It was history in the making, and Teigh and Belle were right there to be a part of it in October 2007. Since the program was new to everyone at the hospital, there were many orientation meetings for the volunteers as well as for the staff. To begin, all of the potential dog handlers had to go through volunteer orientation, health procedures, and background checks, things that any volunteer at MSK had to do. The involvement of the four-legged volunteers required a new level of orientation and instruction, however, and because of our work with our therapy dogs elsewhere, Cheri and I were asked to share our experiences. I showed my Angel On A Leash slide show a few times to let everyone see the kind of impact we hoped to have at MSK with the dogs.

When everything was finally in place, the people in the security office got a kick out of placing each dog on a chair and adjusting the camera so that Teigh Frei and Belle Frei and all of the others could have their pictures taken for their groundbreaking ID cards.

We were ready to go. Among the initial teams approved at MSK, I was the only male handler. Given that we would be visiting the women's health floor, and the patients would be those dealing with female cancer issues, I asked if everyone would be okay with my presence and if there were any psychological barriers that it might create. The reality, of course, is that, male or female, we aren't supposed to talk about anything having to do with the patients' surgeries, treatments, prognoses, and the like. I thought that I could handle it; after all, I am just the guy on the other end of the leash who makes sure that the real stars and therapists —Teigh and Belle—got there. But I wanted to be sure that all concerned had considered that Teigh and Belle's handler was different from everyone else. I got an overwhelming yes, and off we went.

At MSK, a canvasser visits the patients early in the day and finds out if they are interested in a visit from a therapy dog team. The canvasser checks on allergies, fears, roommates, and more, but eventually needs to get a signed release form before adding someone to the list of people for us to visit. The list is a bit fluid because perhaps by the time we get there, certain patients won't be feeling up for a visit because of what they had been through during the day.

So Teigh and I, sporting our new ID badges, showed up, ready to go, on that first evening. We got our visit list from Volunteer Services and headed toward the tenth floor. Tara, the social worker who had designed the program, accompanied us to the tenth floor, but she wasn't going to follow us into the rooms. She was eager to get reports as quickly as we could share them with her, but she didn't want to complicate things by being in the rooms with us.

Teigh, as always, was ready for anything. A pet, a hug, a scratch, a smile, an encouraging word—that's what he lived for. Me, I was thinking that this was going to be productive, and I was excited about expanding our world with a target audience I had not visited before. But my job, as always, was to get Teigh or Belle there, make sure that they were safe, and make sure that they didn't get tangled in any tubes or step on any sutures. Let's get some smiles, have a little conversation, and then head on to the next patient. We'd been in a few hospitals in our time, so I thought that this wouldn't be too much different, even if it was one of the most famous hospitals in the world.

Tara had our first patient picked out and walked us to the room. "Good luck," she said, and she sent us in to make history for MSK.

Generally speaking, we do not go into a room with any specific knowledge of what a patient is going through. We may get some ideas over the course of the visit as we position the dog for hugs and pets, but no one says, "They did this, this, and this to me..."

I was going to play it by the book for this first visit, and I used the same line that I had uttered hundreds of times over the years on my therapy dog visits in many different facilities.

"Hi, Karen. I'm David, and this is my therapy dog Teigh. Is this a good time for a visit?"

The "Hi, Karen" was barely out of my mouth when I looked at the patient, and my heart started to race. A beautiful young blonde woman, Karen was lying in bed, crying and in pain. The way she was holding her arms, I could tell that she was really hurting, and it gave me an idea of what kind of surgery she had just been through. She seemed scared, too, which was no surprise, all things considered.

Take a breath, I told myself. I have to be under control for both Teigh and the patient.

Before she could answer me, I asked another question:

"Are you OK? Do you need a nurse or a social worker or a chaplain?"

"No!" she said emphatically through the tears. "I need you guys; just stay right here."

"We're not going anywhere until you tell us to leave," I said. I was fighting back tears, too, as I thought to myself, No crying, be strong, you're here to help.

Teigh was already at Karen's bedside, his muzzle on the bed. He always seemed to know when he was needed, and he got right to work. Karen reached down to pet him, slowly unfolding her arms and, I hoped, taking her mind off her pain.

I could see that there was room for him on the bed. "How about if we try to get him up there with you?" I asked. "Can we do that?"

"Yes, I'd love that."

So I took the spare sheet that I always travel with and spread it out over her.

"What do I need to know about sutures and tubes and whatever else you have going on? I don't want him causing any problems."

"I've got something up here," she said, pointing to her chest. "Just be careful."

That's one thing about Teigh. He can chase squirrels through Carl Schurz Park like a crazed hunting dog and tear through the apartment like one of them has gotten inside, but when he gets up on that hospital bed, he shuts down his physical side. He knows.

I lifted him up and put him on his back, along her side, with his head resting on her shoulder. She wrapped her arms around him and, still crying, still in pain, broke into a little smile. Me, too.

Karen didn't say anything at that point; she didn't need to. I could hear Billy Matthews, my NBC producer, in my ear, saying, "Lay out, lay out..." (this is what he says to me through my headset when we are on the air and he wants me to let the moment being captured by the shot play itself out). So I kept quiet, too.

Teigh, God love him (one of my oft-uttered phrases when talking or thinking about Teigh), lay there like a rock. He looked her in the eye and occasionally closed his eyes. He was loving it, too.

"He's so good," Karen said to finally break the quiet moment.

"He is very comfortable with you," I told her. "He trusts you totally."

"He's smiling," she said.

"Well, why wouldn't he be?" I said. "You're smiling, too."

"Yes, I guess I am," she said. "The first time in a while. All because of him. And you."

"He's doing all the work; I'm just sitting here, watching you both. It's a wonderful moment."

Teigh and I were in there for probably half an hour. I usually try to move along after ten minutes, give or take. Thirty minutes is a long visit, but I saw no reason to leave her, as we were obviously doing something for Karen's physical pain and her psychological pain. Besides, I had promised her that we would stay there until she told us to leave.

Eventually, Karen said, "Well, I suppose I should let you get to some other patients."

"You aren't holding us against our will," I said, laughing. She smiled, too. What a difference from when we had walked into the room. I lifted Teigh from her bed and set him on the floor. He pushed his face back to Karen on the bed, and she gave him one last two-handed pet and a big smile.

"Thanks so much. I can't tell you how much this did for me," she said, probably more to Teigh than to me. This was a powerful visit, as powerful as any I had ever done.

"We visit here once a week," I told her as we gathered up to leave, giving my usual close for this unusual visit. "Teigh and I loved meeting you and our time together, but I hope that we never see you here again. Go home, be well, Godspeed."

Teigh seemed reluctant to leave the room. We gave Karen one last glance and smile and stepped out of the room.

Tara was waiting for Teigh and me at the nurses' station. "How'd it go?"

"I am exhausted," I told her. "When we walked in the door, she was crying and in pain. When we walked out, she was still crying and in pain, but she was smiling. And so was I. Teigh loved her; he was wonderful. I'm going to call that a great visit for all of us."

"That's a nice start," Tara said. "Let's see who's next on the list."

"Let me catch my breath a bit," I said. "This was very intense. I'll go anywhere and do anything for Karen and others like her; that's why we do this. But as rewarding as it is, Teigh and I can't do more than a couple of visits that intense in one night, or we'll burn out very quickly."

Teigh was lying on the floor, accepting attention and pets from a couple of the nurses.

"I thought she would be a special challenge," Tara said. "That's why we started you with her."

Welcome to Sloan-Kettering. And Sloan-Kettering, welcome to the world of therapy dogs.

• • • • • •

One of the rules for therapy dog work is that you visit in the moment, and you don't take it home with you. That means that you have no further contact with your patients beyond the hospital, outside your visit(s).

I really was curious to find out what happened to Karen. I wanted some assurance that she had made it home and that she went on with her life after her major surgery, but as therapy dog volunteers, we just have to have faith that good things happen, that the surgeries or the treatments were successful, and that the patients go home to good lives.

That's what I did in Karen's case. It's what I hope for with everyone, before and after Karen, through the years. I say a little prayer for all of them. In Karen's case, maybe because she was our very first patient at MSK and because it was such a great visit, I really found myself wanting to know. But it wasn't supposed to happen.

So we were underway at the world-famous Sloan-Kettering, visiting once a week and doing things for people in need. After the initial six months of the pilot program, we expanded into other areas of the hospital.

And then...

In February 2009, I was part of a television show on CNBC called *American Originals: The Westminster Dog Show*. As spokesperson for the club and the "Voice of the Westminster Kennel Club," I was on camera several times, talking about the club, our show, and our history, and about dogs in general. It aired on February 8, the night before our 2009 dog show began.

A week later, while I was going through my post-Westminster email, I came across this:

From: Karen
Sent: Monday, February 16, 2009 12:41 PM
To: David
Subject: Karen—Patient of Sloan-Kettering—Thank you.

David,

I am writing to you, as I have finally learned of your name through a CNBC television program that aired Feb. 8 about the Westminster Dog Show.

I am a patient of Sloan-Kettering in NY, and I was the first patient to have a pet at my side for the introduction of your pet-patient program. You brought a sweet doggie to me on that day in October of 2007 who sat by my side...and I just cried...still trying to deal with my cancer surgery and pain. I could not remember your name but always remembered your face...today I saw you on TV and got your name.

Thank you for taking time to volunteer. The time that you and your doggie spent by my side is a memory that will last for me a lifetime.

Bless you for making my situation just a bit more tolerable.

Karen

Sometimes on my visits, the topic of Westminster comes up. Sometimes, the canvasser will have told patients about what I do in my "other" life, and they will want to talk about the show or their own dogs. Or perhaps someone has watched Westminster or the National Dog Show and seen me on the telecast. I don't believe that was the case with my visit with Karen. It never came up, I never mentioned it; she just came across me on the CNBC show and figured out how to reach me, a year and a half after we had met at the hospital. I am so glad that she did. To have her thank me was nice, but it was more important to me just to hear that she was all right and living her life. I wrote her back:

Karen: Wow. You were the very first patient that Teigh and I visited at MSK after spending most of our previous time as volunteers at the Ronald Mc-Donald House working with kids.

Our visit with you was very emotional. I remember you crying and being in physical pain, and my guess was that you were within 24 hours of having had your surgery. I wanted to do more, but it was obvious that Teigh was taking care of things. At the end of our visit, I saw that you were still crying and still in pain, but you were smiling. Me, too (the crying and the smiling part, plus a little pain in my heart for you).

I have always wondered what happened to you, but I am not allowed to do that. But I did wonder anyway. It means so much to hear from you.

I am so honored and flattered that you took the time to find me and to write. God bless you.

Win the battle; whatever we can do to help, let me know. You're in our hearts and prayers.

Best,

David

That says it all. I was indeed honored and flattered to hear from her. We get lots of thank-yous and wonderful praise when we are visiting, but most of the time that's the end of it. To hear such kind words later lets us know that we really have helped someone.

David,

What a nice surprise and delight getting your email early this morning before work.

I go back to Sloan for my first CAT scan since the operation Friday March 13th. I am hoping for a good outcome. After the scan I will have a break in the day and I would love for another visit from you and Teigh—if you can...?

Please let me know if a visit of this type (not inpatient) will work for you and Teigh on this day. Perhaps you could meet me and my mother at the MSK Rockefeller Outpatient Pavilion on 53rd Street. Let me know what works for you.

I send frequent prayers thanking Teigh for the gift of love and compassion—it is overwhelming.

All smiles and a very heartfelt thank you,

Karen

I was thinking of a great line from *Ghostbusters* when Bill Murray's character, Dr. Venkman, wanted to break a rule that he had just quoted. "Actually, it's more of a guideline than a rule," he shrugged.

> Karen: That works for us. I can bring Teigh, he is now 12 ½ and getting blinder every day, God love him. He doesn't visit much anymore, but I know he will want to see you again.
> Best,
> David

So, I met Karen, her mother, and her friends. She brought a bag of cookies for Teigh and a bag of cookies for me. Pictures and tears and hugs all around. Wow.

> Hi David,
> I wanted to send a note of thanks to you and Teigh—my angel on a leash. It really was my pleasure in having the chance to meet you under very different circumstances. I am all smiles when I have the opportunity to tell my story, and even get to say how we are invited as your guests to the Westminster—what an honor, and so exciting.
> I wanted to share with you the picture from that day, and I threw in two more pictures...I don't have pups, but two wonderful kitties (18+ and 22+ lbs) named Mendel and Watson. I can only hope their pictures will bring a smile to you, as they do for me every day.
> Many, many thanks for your kindness and generosity of your time. I am so very happy knowing there really are wonderful people and their pets doing great things for others—just because.

With kindness and health to you and Teigh,
Warm wishes,
Karen

My response:

Karen: Great to hear from you. I am sorry that I have not already written you to tell you what a wonderful moment it was for both Teigh and me to get to see you again. And we both enjoyed our cookies (I won't tell you whose were gone first).

Thanks for the photos. Your therapy kitties did make me smile, too—it's great what our animals bring to us each and every day.

Best,
David

Sadly, my next email to Karen was to tell her of Teigh's passing in January of 2010. She wrote back:

David,

I am heartbroken. My Teigh was there at a very difficult time in my life, and I only wish I could have returned the favor. What Teigh meant to me:

- Hope and comfort
- Love and smiles
- Warmth and kindness
- Caring and understanding
- Health and wellness

I have a loving memory of Teigh at my bedside

while I was in great pain and so scared. Teigh helped me—a memory and feeling only the two of us will share, and for that I am beyond grateful.

Teigh will always be my forever companion.

I will miss you Teigh, and thank you for such a special memory. David, I am sorry for the loss of your family member. My heart goes out to you.

Karen

Then I got this email right after Westminster 2011:

David,

Wonderful Westminster!!

I think of you often—in fact, your name, Teigh's name, your organization, and our story have become a part of who I am. It is comforting to know that someone who I had never met came to my bedside with a wonderful pet Angel who for no other reason was there for me. It is amazing! They say "everything happens for a reason"… it is not hard to believe in that saying anymore. Teigh and the reason … the reason to believe … maybe I will have a real second chance at life … another chapter of sorts. I keep my eye on the goal—5 yrs or more.

Stay well and keep doing what you are doing … you too are an Angel.

Sincerely,

Karen

"Keep doing what you are doing."
This is why I do what I do.

Angels for Everyone

Angel On A Leash was a big hit from the beginning. It began modestly enough—as a charitable activity for the Westminster Kennel Club at the NewYork-Presbyterian Morgan Stanley Children's Hospital. We were able to share all of it—the patients, the dogs, the handlers, the medical professionals, and the administrators—with the Westminster audience live at the Garden and also live on television, starting in 2005.

The response was huge. We got rousing ovations at the Garden and hundreds of phone calls and emails after the show. People wanted to be part of it; they wanted to get trained, registered, and visiting with their dogs, doing something for people in need in their communities. And the media loved Angel On A Leash, too, doing follow-up stories after the show. Angel On A Leash was truly helping us emphasize that the Westminster Dog Show is indeed a celebration of the dogs in our lives.

After Morgan Stanley Children's Hospital, Ronald McDonald House New York, and Providence Medical

Center in Portland, Oregon, more facilities came to be Angel partners, including Hackensack University Medical Center, New Jersey; Children's Hospital of Wisconsin; New Milford Hospital, Connecticut; St. Jude's Children's Research Hospital, Memphis; Ronald McDonald House of Milwaukee; New Alternatives for Children, New York; Memorial Sloan-Kettering Cancer Center, New York; and the Fisher House at Michael E. DeBakey VA Medical Center, Houston. Ronald McDonald House of Memphis (at St. Jude's); the Children's Hospital at Montefiore, the Bronx, New York; Mid South Therapy Dogs, Memphis; Reading Education Assistance Dogs (R.E.A.D.), Salt Lake City; and the Animal Medical Center, New York, also joined us.

As we were adding facilities, it became evident that Angel should become its own organization. With Westminster's continued support, Angel On A Leash became its own 501(c)(3) charity. Famous New York landlord Newmark Knight Frank contributed office space for us in the Theatre District, and we went to work.

We had a huge reach because of our media exposure, and the phone was ringing every day with people who wanted to become Angel On A Leash therapy dog teams with their dogs in their hometowns. It is difficult, at best, to service individuals in hundreds of cities nationwide, so we decided that our emphasis would be on partnering with facilities to help them create or maintain therapy dog programs shaped by our own distinctive influence and focus. We created a mission statement:

Angel On A Leash champions working with therapy dogs in health care facilities, schools, rehabilitation, hospice, extended care, correctional facilities, and crisis intervention. Through advocacy, education, research, and service, Angel On A Leash promotes the role of the human-canine bond in enhancing human health and quality of life.

From our mission statement, we created the following description of our philosophy, our Margin of Excellence, which helps make Angel On A Leash unique in the field of therapy dogs and animal-assisted interactions:

- Working with facilities to create and support a therapy dog program unique to that facility; a program that meets the needs of its clients and patients; training teams, monitoring their effectiveness, and providing continuing counsel;
- Training the human partner of the team, who drives the experience and must be the guiding hand for the team; preparing them for that experience with our enhanced standards of practice;
- Protecting the dogs as they work, emphasizing that the safety and health of the dog is the top priority for the handler, who must be the constant advocate and protector of the dog;
- Supporting research on the effect of our work on the health and well-being of patients, clients, family, staff, and the volunteers themselves, and the effect of that work on the health of the dogs.

Our guiding principles are constantly being developed and evaluated by Angel On A Leash in association with our partners, which provides a perspective that enhances relationships while helping us build effective and successful programs.

While we weren't able to handle individuals, we still wanted people to get involved with their dogs, wherever they might be. That is our mission, after all—to promote the practice. So we decided to coordinate our program with Delta Society's Pet Partner program, which had about 10,000 individual teams around the country as well as many instructors and evaluators. We would refer inquiring individuals to Delta, where they could get into the therapy dog world. We might not have had an Angel On A Leash partner facility for them in their area, but that was not as important to us as getting the dogs and their humans volunteering and helping people in need.

I am a past board member of and PR consultant for Delta Society, and all of my dogs have been registered with the organization. A number of our Angel board members—including my mentor, Christi Dudzik—have been involved with Delta as well. We are all full believers in what Delta does and how they do it. So we have the best of all worlds—our own perspective and philosophy on the importance of therapy dogs for the facilities, and Delta's teaching programs and registration for the individual teams.

• • • • • •

When Angel On A Leash was expanding into Providence Portland Medical Center in Oregon, I went out there for a press event. My longtime friend, Tom Lasley, an executive at the hospital and a board member of Angel On A Leash, hosted the conference with doctors, pediatric patients, and hospital officials in attendance. Tom brought his wonderful yellow Labrador, Alain, a therapy dog who visits at the hospital, to help us with the "photo opps" for the TV crews and photographers who were there.

After the press conference, the three TV crews followed us upstairs to the cardiac unit to visit a patient, Mr. Ebey. He had been at the hospital for several weeks, recovering from a crisis during open-heart surgery. Alain and Tom had been visiting him for a couple of weeks already, and on this day, we were doing it for the TV crews, to show them what therapy dog visits were like.

Tom told me that this had been a special day for Mr. Ebey, as his endotracheal breathing tube had just been removed and he was breathing on his own. He was sitting up in a chair and seemed quite happy to see Alain, smiling and petting him. After we had been there for a few minutes and the camera crews had gotten their shots, I suggested that we all step out of the room for a break, so as not to get Mr. Ebey too worked up. We retreated out into the hallway; the TV crews, with their task accomplished, departed.

We were standing in the hall with one of the nurses, Lisa, and had only been out of the room for a few minutes when Mr. Ebey slowly lifted his arm and motioned in our direction. Tom looked at me, seemingly surprised to see Mr. Ebey being this active. Then he looked at Lisa.

"This is new; he's been intubated all this time until this morning," Lisa said. "We have never heard him talk; we don't even know if he can."

Tom shrugged his shoulders and said, "Well, let's go see what's on his mind."

Tom handed me Alain's leash, and he and Lisa went back into the room. I waited in the hall and watched. Tom leaned in, and it looked to me as if Mr. Ebey said something to him.

Tom straightened up and broke into a huge grin. He looked at me and took a couple of steps in my direction.

"More dog," Tom said.

Wow. Mr. Ebey had just said the first two words anyone has heard him say in weeks, the first two words that he said after heart surgery, the first two words after finally getting his endotracheal tube removed.

Not "water, please" or "pain pill" or "help me." Out of all the words he could have picked, his first two words were "more dog."

Mr. Ebey lit up, and his wife and nurses were smiling. I was thrilled for Mr. Ebey, for Alain and Tom, and for therapy dogs everywhere. Me, the PR guy, I saw a marketing opportunity unfolding right before my eyes.

"More dog."

• • • • • •

Shortly after that, my friend Jill Rappaport of NBC called and told me that she wanted to do a feature on Angel On A Leash for the *Today Show*. Jill was well known as the red-carpet reporter for *Today*, covering big-time celebrity events like the Oscars, but she was doing more and more animal stories, which was where her heart had always been. She had a great time as the floor reporter for the Westminster telecast in 2006. I was happy for her that the NBC people were letting her follow her heart. She had done some wonderful stories for the network, and away from the studio, she was writing a children's book, *Jack & Jill* (published in 2009), about her rescue dog, Jack, and his battle with cancer.

I'm a PR guy, remember, so I gave the *Today Show* a pretty quick yes. I suggested three places for them to shoot, and Jill took her crew on location.

First, they went to the Morgan Stanley Children's Hospital. There, they shot a couple of our teams—Barbara Babikian and her Sheltie, Lille; and Gay Cropper and her Brussels Griffons, Mr. Gruffyd Babayan—visiting and "bringing smiles and comfort to children and families," as Jill said in the voice-over.

"When you have the opportunity to put a smile on a the face of a child who's not feeling well," Barbara said to Jill, "it's the best feeling in the world." She and Gay and their wonderful dogs are two of our star teams.

From there, it was over to the ASPCA for a look at a therapy dog training class taught by Michele Siegel, one of our most popular instructors. "Visiting is all about knowing your dog, and that's today's focus," Michele told her class on camera. "Every time you interact with people, you're doing good. If you can make them feel better when you are there, that's a good thing and that could be a little miracle."

Back at Morgan Stanley Children's Hospital, Jill spoke to Cynthia Sparer, executive director of the hospital. "Our job is to take care of children who are sick, but children don't stop being children just because they are sick," she told Jill.

"They've learned that treating sick children takes more than medicine," Jill said in my favorite part of her voice-over.

Morgan Stanley Children's Hospital had lined up pediatric oncologist Dr. Kara Kelly to be a part of the shoot, and she told Jill: "I've seen that children are much less stressed when the dogs come into the room. As you can imagine, having medical professionals come in and poke and prod them and examine them is very difficult for them. So having the dog there feels very safe to them; it helps them to forget all the other things that are happening. We'll see a reduction in their heart rate, which is a very sensitive marker in children for stress. It is interesting to see the differences sometimes when the dogs are in the room."

For her final stop, Jill brought her crew to Ronald McDonald House. There, Chaplain Cherilyn Frei, who brings Teigh and Belle to work with her on a regular basis, told Jill that "the dogs are doing good work, and you can just see that by the smiles that light up on the children's faces, the parents', the staff's. Wherever they go, they are doing wonderful work. They are blessed and I am blessed to be the person on the other end of the leash."

It was a great piece, more than six minutes long, and we closed it in the studio with Jill and I visiting live with *Today Show* host Meredith Vieira. Teigh and Belle were with me, looking quite alert and attentive—the world outside the studio couldn't see Cherilyn on the floor behind the cameras, keeping their attention.

Meredith, Jill, and I had a nice discussion about all that we had just seen. Meredith suggested that Jill's dog, Jack, could be a good therapy dog candidate, but Jill expressed some concern about his behavior. It gave me the opportunity to close the segment with one of my favorite expressions: "You know, we worry too much about what we teach our dogs. We need to worry more about what we learn from them, and this is a good program to show just that."

• • • • • •

In 2008, Ronald McDonald House New York and Angel On A Leash were honored with the prestigious Community Partnership Award, given annually by Mutual of America. We got a doggy party—hosted by the Mutual of America Foundation and its president and CEO, Thomas Gilliam—at the New York Athletic Club (NYAC), sharing the moment with our teams and families from the House. I'm not sure how often dogs get to attend functions at the NYAC, but the club has been a gracious host of Angel teams on several occasions. It is also the site for the annual Ronald McDonald House volunteer recognition dinner, and the dogs are always part of that event.

The Mutual of America annual award recognizes "outstanding nonprofit organizations in the United States that have shown exemplary leadership by facilitating partnerships with public, private, or social sector leaders who are working together as equal partners, not as donors and recipients, to build a cohesive community that serves as a model for collaborating with others for the greater good."

This was a perfect description of the relationship that we had with Ronald McDonald House. They had never allowed a dog in the House until we got there with Angel On A Leash, which Cherilyn introduced in 2006, her first year on the job there.

Ronald McDonald House president Bill Sullivan, always saying the right thing and saying it well, told the celebrating group: "Therapy dogs bring good cheer and a sense of normalcy to the children at Ronald McDonald House." Bill is my hero; he battles for every one of the kids who come under his care at the House.

Mutual of America also presented five awards for special contributions to the success of the partnership. Angel On A Leash teams Richard Tegtmeier with Tucker and Gay Cropper with Mr. Gruffyd Babayan were recognized for their dedication to their volunteer work at the House; Michele Siegel of the ASPCA for her tireless efforts in training and registering Angel On A Leash teams through Delta Society; Greer Griffith for her work as Angel's director of programs; and Chaplain Cherilyn Frei, Ronald McDonald House's director of family support, for creating and integrating the therapy dog program at the House.

As part of the celebration later that week, eight of our therapy dog teams rang the ceremonial closing bell for the NASDAQ stock market. Families from the House helped Lille, Belle, Lilly, Mr. Gruffyd Babayan, Fauna, Tucker, Teigh, and Angel ring the bell as Ralph Vogel, director of volunteer services for the House; Thomas Moran, CEO of Mutual of America; and I were the guys in suits representing our organizations.

As it turned out, the ceremony also helped celebrate the biggest one-day gains for stocks in about four months, with the NASDAQ Composite up 7.1 percent and the Dow Jones up 5.8 percent for the day.

Let's give credit where credit is due: the Angel On A Leash teams work little miracles wherever they go!

· · · · · ·

In our first few years of existence, before Angel On A Leash became an independent organization, we were a part of the festivities of the Westminster Kennel Club Dog Show. For a number of years, proceeds from the sale of the annual dog show poster went to Angel.

During the evening competition, Westminster recognized the contributions of Angel On A Leash therapy dog teams in the community. Angel teams; patients and families from Morgan Stanley Children's Hospital, Ronald McDonald House, Hackensack University Medical Center, St. Jude's Children's Research Hospital, and more; and doctors, nurses, and other health care professionals were introduced onto the floor to an enthusiastic response from the packed house at the Garden.

The most enthusiastic response came in 2009 with the introduction of Uno, the 2008 Best in Show-winning Beagle; Jessie Kuebler, a pediatric oncology patient from Ronald McDonald House; and US Marine Lance Corporal Joshua Bleill, who had lost both of his legs in an explosion in Iraq. Uno was doing appearances all over the country for Angel On A Leash, including throwing out the first pitch at a St. Louis Cardinals' baseball game, where Jessie, who lived in St. Louis, accompanied him on the field. Josh was a true American hero who had been visited by Uno when he had been at the Walter Reed Amputee Patient Clinic the previous spring. In fact, Josh had joined the Angel On A Leash board to help coordinate therapy dog programs with military hospitals, and Uno became one of our celebrity "spokesdogs."

People were up on their feet, cheering and crying for

them all. It was a crowd reaction matched only by the response to Westminster's tribute to the search and rescue dogs of September 11 back in 2002.

• • • • • •

The 2009 presentation got the attention of a gentleman named Joe Yanek, who came to our booth at the show the next day and wanted to help us with a grant from the Fluor Foundation to expand what Angel and Uno had done with Josh at Walter Reed. The Fluor Foundation is the philanthropic arm of the Fluor Corporation, a Fortune 500 international engineering firm.

We did a little research and proposed a therapy dog program for the Fisher House at the Michael E. DeBakey VA Medical Center in Houston, home of the Fluor Corporation's largest corporate headquarters. The Fisher Houses are homes away from home for families of patients receiving medical care at VA and other major military medical centers around the country. They are somewhat similar to Ronald McDonald Houses, with housing fees for the military members underwritten by the Fisher House Foundation.

The Fluor grant focuses on supporting the rehabilitation of our wounded military while also supporting their family members. We staged workshops in Houston and got a number of volunteer Angel teams—employees from Fluor Corporation's Houston Center and their dogs—to work quite quickly.

This was great. It represented a new audience for us, and we were thrilled to be able to create a program to reach our military heroes and their families. We thank the Fluor Foundation for its generous, continued support, and we especially thank Joe for making it happen.

• • • • • •

In 2009, Angel On A Leash was part of a history-making event on the weekend before Westminster with its first ever Angel On A Leash Best In Show benefit, a beautiful event hosted by Ruth Pereira at the Affinia Manhattan Hotel across the street from Madison Square Garden. It was the greatest assembly of show dogs ever in one place, with five Westminster Best in Show winners dating back to 2001. The attendees got to see Uno, the Beagle (2008); James, the English Springer Spaniel (2007); Rufus, the Colored Bull Terrier (2006); Spice Girl, the Miniature Poodle (2002); and JR, the Bichon Frise (2001). Never had so many Westminster Best in Show dogs been in the same place at the same time.

They all looked to me as if they could still run right into the show ring. The party was sold out and attracted media from New York and the dog show world, resulting in coverage from the *New York Times*, MSNBC, the Associated Press, Animal Planet, and more.

The Best in Show Benefit was back at the Affinia in 2010, hosted again by Ruth in a sold-out room. In 2011, with so many of the dogs hitting senior-citizen status, the party was changed to an awards affair for current Angel On A Leash teams. Ruth's party has become a wonderful annual event that we all have come to anticipate with great excitement every February.

In 2011 as well, an additional event was staged as an Angel On A Leash benefit. "Big City, Little Dog" was staged at the New Yorker Hotel and featured a fashion show for local celebrities and their dogs. New York City's New Yorkie pet apparel dressed the runway pups in its new spring line. Schmitty the Weather Dog and meteorologist Ron Trotta (the official weather team for the Westminster Kennel Club Dog Show) were among the New York personalities and celebrities who walked the runway to raise money for Angel On A Leash.

Elly McGuire and Ron chaired the event with huge support from the New Yorker Hotel. As my Aunt Caroline always wrote in her letters, a good time was had by all.

Angel has also enjoyed a number of other unique fundraisers through the years. For example, America's top ballroom dancers were the stars of "Ballroom Unleashed" in 2010, a beautiful event produced by Melanie LaPatin and Tony Meredith, the acclaimed choreographers of *So You Think You Can Dance*. From 2006 to 2009, Doyle New York Gallery's chairman and CEO Kathleen M. Doyle and senior vice president Louis Webre hosted a champagne brunch benefit in their private preview of the gallery's annual "Dogs in Art" sale. And in 2008, the second-grade class at New York City's PS 87, taught by Bebe Morrissey, produced a successful walkathon in Central Park.

· · · · · ·

Every fall, Ronald McDonald House New York holds a block party in its Upper East Side neighborhood to share its work and its accomplishments with the neighbors. The therapy dog program is always a big part of the event. We had our own table, and we would tell people about our work at the House and recruit new volunteers. Cherilyn would always put on a blessing of the animals, and that brought out a lot of the neighbors and their pets.

In 2010, Cherilyn helped engineer the proclamation of New York State Therapy Dog Day for October 2, the day of the block party. The proclamation, presented by State Senator Liz Krueger, recognized the partnership of Ronald McDonald House New York and Angel On A Leash in providing a therapy dog program for the young pediatric oncology patients and their families.

The proclamation by State Senator Krueger read:

WHEREAS, Ronald McDonald House of New York, Inc., provides a temporary "home-away-from-home" for pediatric cancer patients and their families in a supportive and caring environment, which encourages and nurtures the development of child-to-child and parent-to-parent support systems; and

WHEREAS, Ronald McDonald House of New York, Inc., is the largest facility of its type in the world; and

WHEREAS, on October 2nd, 2010, Ronald McDonald House of New York is hosting its Third Annual Block Party, featuring food, live music, entertainment, safety awareness, health screenings, and educational programs, on East 73rd Street between First and York Avenues; and

WHEREAS, the Ronald McDonald House New York–Angel On A Leash program provides therapy dogs for pediatric cancer patients and their families; and

WHEREAS, Angel On A Leash enhances health and quality of life through play and enrichment activities which promote the human-animal bond, and

WHEREAS, therapy dogs help boost morale, self-esteem, and overall feelings of well-being for those dealing with chronic and life-threatening illnesses; and

WHEREAS, studies have shown that petting a dog releases beneficial hormones into the bloodstream known to be associated with healing and feelings of well-being; and

WHEREAS, by initiating and maintaining the relaxation response, pets take a person's focus off of their pain and elevate their mood; and

WHEREAS, children who spend time with pets develop higher levels of empathy and learn responsibility; and

WHEREAS, therapy dog programs such as Angel On A Leash are deserving of recognition for their contributions to the health and well-being of New Yorkers; therefore be it

RESOLVED, that I, State Senator Liz Krueger declare that October 2nd, 2010, is hereby recognized as New York State Therapy Dog Day.

• • • • • •

Morgan Stanley Children's Hospital is a great hospital and a great partner for Angel On A Leash. It is where the program was born with Westminster back in 2004, and today it is ranked among the top children's hospitals in the nation. NewYork-Presbyterian is among the top ten hospitals in the country and is the top-ranked hospital in the metropolitan New York area.

In the early days, when proceeds from the sale of the Westminster poster were earmarked for Angel On A Leash, the hospital hosted a great event each year for the unveiling of the poster. The previous year's Best in Show dog would make an appearance and help with the celebration and photo opps. Josh (Newfoundland, 2004), Carlee (German Shorthaired Pointer, 2005), Rufus (Colored Bull Terrier, 2006), and Uno (Beagle, 2008) got a lot of attention and flashes for Westminster, the hospital, and the therapy dog program through the years. The Angel On A Leash teams who volunteered regularly at the hospital would also attend, making it a canine-rich day at Morgan Stanley Children's Hospital.

The highlight of each year's event was the gathering of the children in the hospital's Winter Garden in the ground-floor lobby. To see them react to the dogs was a treat for all, from the media to the parents to the hospital staff and medical professionals. This was a great illustration of the principles that make therapy dogs effective at their jobs—and what a bonus for Angel On A Leash to have some of the world's top pediatricians on hand to talk to the media about what they saw every day with the dogs and the children. We can talk about the intuitive feelings and the feel-good stuff all day long, and while it makes sense and it works, it's nice to hear the medical professionals talk about it in their terms, too.

The event in the Winter Garden was often broadcast via closed-circuit television to the children in the hospital who could not attend in person. Then, afterward, the dogs would head up to the patients' floors to visit them. The attention to detail, with Toni Millar, the hospital's director of child life, leading the way, was amazing and made the event not only fun but also beneficial for the children and families.

NY1, the New York television news channel, selected Angel On A Leash as its New Yorker of the Week in February 2009 and shot teams visiting at Morgan Stanley Children's Hospital. The *New York Daily News* did a feature about the program, Animal Planet shot on location a couple of times, and George Michael's nationally syndicated *Sports Machine* traveled up to the hospital to shoot a feature. Our Morgan Stanley Children's Hospital volunteer teams were visible in the community at street fairs, block parties, events in Central Park, and other media opportunities all over town. Delta Society shot a public-relations video at the hospital and even held a board meeting on site.

A number of our volunteers were honored for their work at Morgan Stanley Children's Hospital. Greer Griffith, Angel On A Leash program director, was honored at the United Hospital Fund's 16th Annual Hospital Auxilian and Volunteer Achievement Awards ceremony in 2009, joining honorees who had been chosen from among New York City's more than 50,000 health care volunteers from hospitals throughout the five boroughs.

I am very proud of Greer, and we are lucky to have her with Angel. She has always been a great warrior for therapy dogs in general and Angel On A Leash in particular. Greer and her black Labs, Clayton and Fauna, were among the first teams to make therapy visits to the Family Assistance Center at Ground Zero (Pier 94) following the 9/11 terrorist attacks. Greer has been very involved with New Alternatives for Children, a New York City agency that supports children with special needs, and before that, she was involved in hippotherapy (therapy horses) for kids participating in the Special Olympics.

When Westminster approved the Angel On A Leash therapy dog program, I grabbed Greer immediately to be our director of programs, a job she has held ever since. Her late husband, Richard, was on our board for many years as well; we miss him dearly.

I also had the good fortune to have three of the country's top therapy dog experts—Christi Dudzik, Mary Ehrhart, and Dr. Stephanie LaFarge—say yes to me when I asked them to join the Angel board. My other current board members, Chuck Bessant, Ranny Green, and Tom Lasley, bring us a lot, too, and we are all working hard to get Angel On A Leash doing all of the things that we'd like it to do.

66 *Give them a chance to talk and smile and laugh, and you might just make their day. They might make yours, too.* **99**

CHAPTER 7

Therapy on the Street

A straight line is the shortest distance between two points. Pythagoras, or whatever geometric whiz came up with that one, never had a dog.

When the weather was right, I would walk one of the dogs to my Westminster office, just a little less than 3 miles from my apartment, as the taxi travels. But, as the dog walks, it was certainly more than 3 miles. It's a forty-five minute walk without a dog; with a dog, it's at least an hour. That straight-line stuff applies only to a dog's route to his food bowl.

Belle would be at the door, ready to go. She seemed to sense when I was going to take her to work with me. I'm not sure if it had something to do with the weather or some vibe I was giving off, but she knew. I'm guessing that it was the vibe. After all, that's what she was working from when she did her therapy dog thing, and she was so good at that.

By now, Teigh was more into walking the couple of blocks over to Finnegan's Wake for dinner on the sidewalk. He was slowing down in his life, so it was just Belle and me most of the time. A few times, I walked both of them to the office, but it was a lot of work walking two dogs that far. Often I would arrive at the office looking as if I had run those 3 miles, in need of a shower at the end of a workout.

Add to all of this the fact that many New Yorkers don't understand and appreciate, as we did, the importance of walking two dogs on the sidewalk in the city during rush hour. We tried it a couple of times, but eventually I took to heart the ever-so-polite suggestions of some of the locals that perhaps we should not be taking up so much space on their sidewalks. So it became "Take Your Daughter to Work Day" most of the time—just Belle and me.

Belle actually had a nice history of coming to work with me, dating back to my days in Seattle. At the time, Cheri and Teigh were a registered therapy team, and they would be visiting somewhere a couple of days a week, working for Healing Paws. Belle would come to the office with me, as we were not yet a registered therapy team.

I had an office on a marina on Lake Union that I rented from a yacht brokerage; it was the greatest office I ever had. My doors opened right onto the dock, and Belle had a great time chasing the geese off the dock, something much appreciated by the locals who lived there on their boats.

Brittanys—at least my Brittanys—are not particularly big water dogs. Belle wouldn't intentionally jump in, but I had to fish her out of the water a couple of times. The first time was when she decided that she was going to chase a duck and her ducklings that were swimming by. As I watched Belle run right off the end of the dock, it appeared to me that she thought she was going to run out onto the water and play with them all. *Ker-splash*! It was quite funny, and I was still laughing as I pulled her back onto the dock, explaining to her the concept of a body of water and wondering if she had somehow heard the stories about Moses and Jesus and water from her mother, the chaplain-in-waiting.

Another time, she was about to jump off the dock onto the back of one of the yachts that was moored right in front of my door. She started to jump, and I shouted at her just as she launched herself into the air. It was like a scene out of a Road Runner cartoon, where Wile E. Coyote is momentarily frozen in midair and has a helpless look on his face as he realizes that disaster is imminent.

So Belle E. Coyote looked over her shoulder at me, and I swear she was in a cartoon still frame. Then she dropped straight into the water, *ker-splash* again, just short of her target.

So, what do you have for me today, Belle? What is our next adventure? Just setting out with her on the journey was enough to bring a smile.

Our usual route was to head west on 72nd Street and turn south on Park Avenue to Midtown. The sidewalks, generally speaking, are wider and cleaner on Park on the Upper East Side, and there is no commercial traffic allowed, no subways, and no buses, so it's a little quieter.

Of course, we got the usual amount of social opportunity along the way from dogs and their humans. Sometimes these encounters turned into chances for me to tell people about therapy dog work and invite them to get involved in a class. Sometimes we had to dodge a snarling Napoleon-complexed small dog or an overly romantic large male. Or maybe we met some eccentric types who wanted to share their history in dogs with us or tell us how the mayor has wronged them or divulge that they lived next door to some celebrity who partied too much.

Belle loved them all. It was fun for me, too, but chances are that I wouldn't have stopped or had conversations with any of them if it weren't for Belle. It's true of all of my dogs—they bring people into my life. And the next time I'm walking down that street, maybe without a dog, I just might stop and talk with them again.

At 60th Street and Park Avenue, there is a beautiful big stone church. There's a courtyard on the north side of the church that is the unlikely overnight accommodation to a few homeless guys who sleep there on cardboard. If we walked by early enough, they would be starting to stir.

The first time we walked by, we heard a whistle. Belle and I looked up at the same time and saw a man sitting on his cardboard. He whistled again and called her: "Come here, girl!"

She was at the end of the lead immediately and in his weathered face as fast as I could get her there. He gave her a big hug and started petting and scratching her. Belle was immediately his for life.

"What a good girl," he said with a subdued smile. "How does she do with birds?"

"Pretty good," I answered. "But she doesn't see too many pheasants around here. Even on Park Avenue, the city bird of choice is still the pigeon, and she points them all."

He laughed as Belle started to push her hind end at him for some more scratches.

"I used to have a great bird dog," he said. "He looked kinda like her, only darker and he was bigger."

"Did you hunt with him?"

"Yeah, a little..." His voice trailed off. He was probably somewhere in his past, in a field with his dog. Wherever his mind was taking him, it made him smile. Me, too.

Belle knew that all of these guys wanted to see her. She was always eager to make the rounds here, and just about every one of them had something for her—a pet, a scratch, a hug, some nice words. She went to as many of them as she could find. I don't know who got the bigger kick out of it, Belle or the guys, who probably all needed something to smile about.

Not to sound too trite, but to me it seemed a little bit magical. These are people who I probably would have just walked right past on a normal day in my previous life. Over time, though, Belle taught me that they had something to offer us both, whether it was an observation about Park Avenue, thoughts on the New York weather, or wise words about life in general.

The lesson learned was that these guys had lives, too, and stories to tell if you would hang in there long enough. Give them a chance to talk and smile and laugh, and you might just make their day. They might make yours, too. I think I can speak for Belle in saying that usually we both left there feeling good.

At some point, we had to get off Park Avenue before it went under the MetLife Building at 46th Street. One morning, we turned onto 51st Street, crossed Madison Avenue and continued to Fifth Avenue. The Westminster office is on Madison, but I wanted to walk on Fifth Avenue, as it is a little roomier. There were more people, so I just had to keep Belle close and protect her from being stepped on.

Belle could cause a traffic jam on the Fifth Avenue sidewalks because the people in business suits would stop for their morning dose of canine therapy, too. And you know what? The encounters with the suits weren't much different from the encounters with the cardboard guys in the courtyard at the church. The only difference was that these people were dressed a little better and were rushing to get somewhere. But they were smiling when they walked away, too, even if they had to brush off a little dog hair from those suits.

I always tried to get a morning look at the world-famous St. Patrick's Cathedral, a historical Catholic church that sits between 51st and 50th Streets and between Madison and Fifth Avenues. One morning, Belle and I actually went into the church during morning Mass and sat in the back. The security people looked at us but let us pass. When it came time for Holy Communion, I walked up to the front of the church with Belle (she came along for the long walk up the aisle). I had never done that before, and I haven't done it since. We wanted to be respectful, but I didn't want to leave her tied up in the pew.

After Mass, back out on the sidewalk, Belle led me to someone, and I was visiting with him when I realized that she was already elsewhere at the end of the leash. I turned and found her with her head on the lap of an older gentleman in a wheelchair. He was petting her and laughing, getting the biggest kick out of her.

"What a beautiful dog," he said. "What's her name?"

"This is Belle," I said, "and I'm David, Belle's dad."

"Well, hello, Belle and David. How nice to meet you. My name is Robert."

We were in Robert's marketing area. He had his chair in a strategic, busy location, in the middle of the traffic flow at the corner of 50th and Fifth, right in front of the church. He was obviously a "regular" at this location, as many of the people who walked by greeted him by name.

Robert was an elderly (seventy-eight) black gentleman with a bad right eye, a few missing teeth, a hat that read "Jesus Saves," and a small American flag attached to the back of his chair. He had a large paper cup on his lap, and he shook it every once in a while to remind people that he was there. Right now, however, he was giving Belle everything she was demanding. She loved it, and so did he.

"She's so beautiful," he said.

"Well, I would have to agree," I replied. "And she obviously loves you. Whatever you're doing, don't stop."

"Hi Bobby," a woman said, dropping a few coins into his cup.

"God bless you," he called to her.

"What kind of a dog is she?"

"She's a Brittany, a bird dog."

Someone else stuffed a dollar into the cup and said, "Have a good day."

"Thank you. God bless you," said Robert.

Back to Belle: "She's beautiful." She was standing on her hind legs with her front legs on his lap and her nose in his face, giving him a little kiss.

I chatted with him a little, finding out that he lived over on Amsterdam Avenue. He tried to keep a regular schedule here, but it was obviously very dependent on the weather. He told me that he was an Army veteran and was tickled to find out that I was, too.

He never stopped smiling. He threw out "God bless yous" and "Jesus loves yous" to everyone who looked at him, talked to him, patted him on the shoulder, or dropped something in his cup.

That morning, Belle and I had a little something extra in our step as we headed down Fifth Avenue toward the office—just as we did every time we bumped into Robert on the street over the next few years.

· · · · · ·

Before the 2008 Westminster show, Saks Fifth Avenue and Westminster partnered to build a display for several of the Saks windows in the store on 50th Street and Fifth Avenue. Saks dedicated some of its windows to our show, and we helped the store put a nice display together that was in place for a two-week span before, during, and after the show.

We took James, the wonderful English Springer Spaniel who had won Best in Show the previous year (2007) to Saks on the Friday afternoon before the show for a media event that was covered by photographers, video crews, and reporters. As we stood outside at the windows, who came rolling up in his wheelchair? Robert. Remember, we were on his turf.

"Hey, David, what are you all doing here?"

I explained the event to him and showed him the media load that was with us. "Why don't you hang out and watch us for a while?"

As all of the Saks suits looked on in wonderment, I rolled Robert closer. He was smiling and enjoying it all. Some of his street "customers" walked by and said hi. "What are you doing, Robert?" one of them asked. "I'm watching this famous dog be on TV," he said proudly.

I saw Robert a few more times that summer, once with Belle and a couple of times when it was just me, and then I lost him for a while. We seemed to be on different schedules because I could never catch him at the church, and that worried me a little bit. Finally, the following spring, Belle and I found him right where he was supposed to be. We had a great visit, as most of our visits with him were.

Not long after that, Belle's health failed, and after a short, valiant battle, she passed (June 2009). Cheri and I were devastated, and we turned ourselves to devoting a lot of time and energy to keeping Teigh alive as he fought the same battle.

One morning, a couple of weeks after Belle's passing, I got on a different bus from home. I got off at 57th and Fifth and then walked to St. Patrick's. I was going there to light a candle for Belle, thinking about how she had actually attended a Mass there with me and had gone up to the main altar with me for Holy Communion. I was also hoping to see Robert.

There was no sign of him when I arrived, so I walked into the church and sat down, said a little prayer for Belle, lit a candle, and walked back out the door, headed to the office. And who was sitting there on the corner outside the church but my friend Robert, in his wheelchair, with his American flag, a donation cup in his lap, and his red hat that read "Jesus Saves." He still wasn't seeing too well, but he was smiling and happy to have someone to chat with.

"How's Belle?" he asked me. I told him that one of the reasons I had come to the church this morning was to try to find him so I could share with him the sad news that she had passed on.

He shed a little tear. "She's in a good place now," he said. He repeated that a few times as we chatted about her for several minutes. I had brought a couple of pictures of her for him—big ones that I knew he could see. I promised him that I would get back to the neighborhood and see him again soon.

If I hadn't had a relationship with Robert because of Belle, I probably would not have stopped to chat with him that day. As it turned out, he was smiling when I walked away. And so was I.

I knew that somewhere, Belle was watching. There is no doubt in my mind that she had made sure that Robert would be there for me—and me for him—on this day.

• • • • • •

I found Robert again a few months later, in the fall, and told him that we were going to get a new puppy to carry on for Belle.

"Bring her to me when you get her," he said. "I hope she's as nice as Belle."

"We hope so, too," I said. "You can help us train her."

It wasn't until the following spring that Grace was old enough to make the trip to the office with me; and even then she still had to ride in a Sherpa bag for much of the journey. But she came out of the bag to be introduced to

Robert, and she sat on his lap for a few minutes, getting some hugs and pets from him and a few of his people.

"She's beautiful," he said. "Grace, you look just like Belle. I hope you are as nice as her."

To me, that seemed like a proper anointing, a passing of the torch from Belle to Grace. It was a Fifth Avenue ceremony, presided over by Robert. Once again, I couldn't help but think that, somewhere, Belle was watching.

66 *Thank you for bringing all your dogs to see me and all the other children. It makes me really happy.* **99**

–GEORGE YEOMANS
AGE 9, RESIDENT AT
RONALD MCDONALD HOUSE

In the Moment

If anyone lives life in the moment, it's a child with cancer. And that child's parents.

Ronald McDonald House New York is a home away from home for kids and their families who have come to New York City to get help in their battles with cancer. This "Ronald House" is dedicated exclusively to pediatric oncology, although other Ronald Houses around the world (nearly 300 of them) may have other missions as well.

In New York, one night's stay at the House is $35, and for most families, the fee is paid by a charity, a hospital, or friends. For some of these families, who spend weeks or months or even years here, that's crucial. The family must have a referral from the social workers at their hospital to be eligible for a stay at the House, where the eighty-four rooms are filled every night.

The children know that they are sick. They may not know exactly why, but they know that they don't feel well and they know that this is why they are here. What can be confusing to them is why, if they are here to get better, the treatments are often so rough on them.

Many of the families have already exhausted treatment options locally or regionally, and they have come to New York for clinical trials in the hope of curing or at least managing their children's cancers. The kids and their families have been through a lot already, and whether they come from Long Island or Indiana or California or Peru or Greece, they are here in New York City because they feel that this is the best hope for their children—a relationship with one of the foremost cancer treatment centers in the world, such as Memorial Sloan-Kettering, New York University Langone Medical Center, or the NewYork-Presbyterian Morgan Stanley Children's Hospital.

It's not easy for the children when they are here, and many of them, sadly, will not be cured. Families face challenges that go beyond the sick children. The disease creates tremendous stress in so many ways within the family unit—between spouses; with healthy siblings, who can feel overlooked; with jobs; with finances; and more. What it really comes down to, however, is this, a straightforward mantra that I hear all the time from Bill Sullivan, the president/CEO of Ronald McDonald House New York: "When a child is sick, the parents are sick."

Those perfect words of Bill Sullivan echo constantly in my mind as I work with the kids and my dogs. If I can make the kids smile, I can make the parents smile. If I can keep the kids' attention for a while, I give the parents a break and maybe even give them the chance to visit with other parents and talk about their challenges, share some knowledge, or at least offer some support and encouragement.

This is a very special place, and I am proud to say that Cheri has been its chaplain and director of family support since 2006. Bill Sullivan is one of my favorite people and the kind of CEO that every health care facility needs. Cheri was one of his first hires when he became president, and he is constantly extolling the importance of what she brings to the House.

One of the things that she brought was a therapy dog program—dogs had never been allowed in the House before. She named it Angel On A Leash, as part of our organization, and the program at the House has been a stellar example of how to do things right and what therapy dogs can bring to a health care facility. Mr. Sullivan, the people on his board, and the Ronald McDonald House staff began as interested observers of the work that the therapy dogs and their human partners do, and they have become the program's greatest fans and supporters—and that helps the program be successful and effective.

The dogs are a big hit. Ronald McDonald House wants to create a family atmosphere, and for many of these families, the dogs help do just that. Many of the families leave their own dogs behind when they come to the House, and that often gives special meaning to the visit and a starting point for conversation. Their dogs are part of their families, and the kids miss them. As it is with patients in any setting, it is often easy to identify those who have dogs—their confidence in approaching them, the way they pet or scratch them, the way they engage them.

"I have a dog," said Laura as she petted my Cavalier King Charles Spaniel, Angel, one evening.

"You do? What kind of dog do you have?"

"A big one," she answered.

I looked up at her father. "A black Lab," he said.

"What's his name?" I asked Laura.

"Max."

"Max is a big dog. Angel could probably run right underneath him, couldn't she?"

Laura kept her hands on Angel. "Yes," she said, nodding quietly.

Cheri and Ronald McDonald House have strict rules for the program, which is so important. The rules are for the dogs and their people and are made first and foremost with the children in mind. Those rules include vaccine protocols and annual health checks for the dogs, registration of each team as a Delta Society Pet Partner, proof of age for the dog, and at least one year of experience as a team visiting in another health care facility. The dogs that visit as volunteers probably have stricter requirements than the human volunteers do! And the human part of the team has to meet the volunteer requirements for the facility, as well—health checks, background checks, orientation, and more.

The dogs are at the House as part of the care program. While the dogs can be entertainers, a therapy dog program is not the circus; this is not what therapy dog work is about. Therapy dogs are a serious part of the services that a facility has to offer its patients and, in the case of Ronald McDonald House, their families as well. Everyone has to play by the rules for the program to be credible and for the children and families to get the most out of it.

The dogs must be trained, and, more importantly, their human partners must be trained, too. The handlers need to protect their dogs at all times, and they need to protect the patients as well. The human half of each team needs to be attentive and anticipatory, always ready for the next challenge, whether it is a child who is a little too enthusiastic, or a dog who is about to step on someone's sutures. I need to be ready for every move that my dog is about to make. To do that, I need to know my dog and I need to be attentive at every moment.

For example, I try not to use treats to motivate my dogs in the facility for two reasons. First, it can make them a little excitable, which often leads to problems, as excitable or overly eager dogs can seem to get themselves into trouble. Second, I don't want my dogs to be looking at me all the time for treats; I want them watching the patients and paying attention to the people in need.

On our "Ronald House" visits, we like to set up in the front lobby, where we have a shot at everyone coming and going as well as people who are just hanging out. The lobby works well because it's easy for all concerned. The kids can be as involved as they want to or when they feel like it. Sometimes we catch families coming back from checkups or treatments or hospital stays. Sometimes they are checking in; sometimes they are just enjoying some downtime. Sometimes they just look down into the lobby from the second and third floors and see the dogs, and they come down to join us.

These kids often are coming back to the House after a tough day or a tough time in the hospital. If they have had some treatment or another round of clinical trials or surgery or a bone-marrow transplant, they may not feel well at all. Sometimes they just keep going to the elevator and on up to their rooms. Most of the time, though, the kids want some of what the dogs have to offer.

"That's the first time he has smiled today," say many parents as they watch their children interact with the dogs. And then the parents break into smiles themselves.

Sometimes a child will ask to take a dog for a walk. "Can I hold the leash?" We're ready with a double-leash setup in which the handler keeps control with one leash and gives the other one to the child, and off we all go.

Sometimes a child needs that walk for physical therapy. Christina, a young girl from Greece, was battling spinal cancer and was reluctant to take a step. One night, she grabbed Teigh's leash, left her crutches behind, and off we went around the lobby—slowly, but Christina nonetheless moved under her own power, with Teigh and me in tow. It may not have been a miracle, but it wasn't something that she had been doing, either.

Christina's physical therapist was there that night. "I have been trying to get her to do that for a week," the therapist told me. "In five minutes, the dog got her to do what I have been begging her to do since last Monday."

This came as no surprise to me. The dog makes things fun. A range-of-motion exercise can be painful and boring, but put a dog in front of the child, put a brush in her hand, and watch what happens. She brushes the dog and does the exercise that the therapist has been looking for, and she does it with a smile on her face.

Another time, we put the dog a few steps away from Michael, a heretofore reluctant walker, and watched him take a few steps to the dog to deliver a treat. "We have been working on him for weeks to do that, and it never happened," his mother told me.

Again, we aren't claiming to be miracle workers, but

the dogs can motivate the patients in so many ways, creating fun situations that make the kids want to work.

I brought Teigh to the House one evening for his regular visit, but he had just undergone minor eye surgery in which the doctor removed a little tumor from his eyelid. He was all sutured up and wearing one of those "cones" around his neck so he couldn't scratch at the sutures.

Well, that was a night that we all had something to talk about. To begin with, the kids got it. A lot of them have had their own surgeries, after all. So they were particularly gentle and sympathetic as they heard the story of Teigh's surgery.

"Was it cancer?"

No surprise that this was the first question. I explained that, yes, it was a little growth, and they had gotten it all.

"Good, they got all of mine, too."

"Can he see?"

I told them yes, pointing out that in spite of the sutures, his eye was open. I explained that the growth had been bothering his eye and that he had been starting to scratch at it.

"What is this for?"

I explained that the cone would keep Teigh from scratching at the area.

"Was he asleep?"

I assured them that he had been asleep for the procedure and showed them where the IV had gone into his leg.

"Me, too, when they did mine."

"Do his stitches itch?"

Apparently, because he acts like they do.

"Me too, it makes me crazy!"

So, these little exercises don't have to be physical. Talk to the dog.

"Can you say hi to Belle?" I asked.

Josh, who never talks, is suddenly babbling away, relatively speaking: "Hi Belle."

I asked him if he had dogs.

"Yes, I have Chihuahuas."

"What are their names?"

"Taco and Chico."

"What color are they?"

We talked for several minutes. His mom was standing behind him, beaming. "He doesn't talk to anyone."

George, a young boy from Greece, initially wasn't sure about dogs. The first time he saw Belle from across the room, he stayed there all night. The following week, he snuck up on us, touched Belle, and then ran back across the room, where he stayed for the rest of the evening. The next week, he was hanging with us for the duration. It wasn't long before he was asking for the leash and the chance to walk her himself.

Cheri tells me that a kid will often peek into her office during the day. "No 'Hello, Chaplain Frei, how are you today?' she says. It's 'Are the dogs coming tonight'?"

Most evenings, the dog will draw a crowd, and that creates a couple of dynamics. First, the handler, responsible for his or her dog's safety and well-being, needs to be sure that the dog is tolerating it all. Each dog is different. Teigh and Belle, and now Grace, are Brittanys and sporting dogs—they put up with the pokes and prods and body slams, the screams and all of the other noise.

I think it's just the nature of the breed; that's what makes them great family dogs and great hunting dogs, unflappable.

As a handler, you need to know your dog. Angel, my little princess of a Cavalier King Charles Spaniel, needed some adjustment time and a little more protection. She has come to love it all, too, but I still have to be protective of her. She loves the kids, but she doesn't love having six of them in her face at once. The bottom line is that she is a wonderful, gentle, unimposing presence with the children, who need someone to hug or pet or talk to.

Many of the kids are "regulars" for the therapy dog visits, even when they may not be feeling great. We always need to be sensitive to the fact that a child may have just had some type of treatment that hurts while it's helping. Maybe today he is wearing a mask because his white cell count is low. Maybe this horrible disease has gotten the best of her today in her daily battle. So tonight, they just don't feel like hanging out with us.

I know that Laura, George, Anthony, Maria, Dylan, Andrea, and so many more kids would always put in appearances with us every Tuesday night, no matter how their days had gone.

"Jessie St. Louie" is the way that Bill always greeted one of the kids, an eleven-year-old girl from St. Louis. Jessie loved the dogs and was always there for the therapy dog visits whenever she was in town. She also got to know Uno, the inimitable Beagle that was Best in Show at the 2008 Westminster show. Uno visited the House with me, first as a celebrity and then as a therapy dog. He was registered with me as his partner after we went through the training together with Michele Siegel. When

Uno and I went to St. Louis so he could throw out the first pitch for a Cardinals game in the summer of 2008, we took Jessie on the field with us for some help.

The following February, Jessie was part of a Westminster presentation on the floor at the Garden. Uno was being recognized for all of his adventures in the year after going Best In Show, which included visiting the White House and Walter Reed Army Medical Center, riding on a float in the Macy's Thanksgiving Day Parade, visiting Ronald McDonald Houses all over the country, and much more. Jessie was included as one of Uno's special friends.

Jessie was a warrior, as are all of these kids, but she packed more into her life than any healthy person could have done. Rock stars, wrestlers, professional athletes—they all knew and loved Jessie. When she passed after her nine-year fight with neuroblastoma, she left with a full resume.

Dylan came to the House from Australia. He arrived in 2005 after his parents had been told that he had six months to live. He's been a special kid to us, and his family—his older brother, Cain, and his parents, Melissa and Tim—have been the heart and soul of the House over these years. Dylan is always there for the dogs, and the dogs are always there for him. Once, after a very difficult and painful oral surgery, he was hurting. His mom suggested that he take Teigh for a walk to see if that would help. He did, and he reported that the walk got his mind off of the pain.

Andrea was fighting a tumor that involved her vertebrae, and she gradually was being paralyzed. That didn't stop her from making every therapy dog night, though.

She was a special friend of Angel and Mr. Gruffyd Babayan (the Brussels Griffon who visited with handler Gay Cropper), and she got a big kick out of Uno.

Andrea and Dylan had a private audience with the Pope when he visited New York City in 2008, and the two of them were pictured in the *New York Post* with Angel as they talked of their anticipation of meeting His Holiness.

Dylan battles on; sadly, Andrea passed in 2010. Too many of them do.

One of our favorite young boys asked to have Angel in bed with him as his dying wish, so she was there as he was taking his last breaths. Yes, that was tough.

One of the kids wrote a letter about his love for the dogs at the House:

My Doggies at Ronald McDonald House
By George Yeomans
Age 9
My name is George Yeomans. I have been staying at the house since the end of May. The one thing I really love about staying here is all the dogs that come to visit. I enjoy seeing all the dogs and giving them cuddles. Some of them can do tricks, like shake and roll over. They are all such nice dogs. They make me feel happy.

I know the names of all the dogs. They are Butter and Serafina, Teigh and Belle, Parker, Phoebe, Tucker, and Mr. Gruffyd Babayan. I know all the types of dogs that they are. I remember Phoebe is a Pomeranian because I think of a pomegranate!

Thank you for bringing all your dogs to see

me and all the other children. It makes me really happy. The lady behind the desk in the lobby, Christine, always rings me up to tell me when the dogs are here. So I only miss them when I am at the hospital.

I had to leave my puppy behind, at home in England, with my Granny. I miss England but I try not to think about it. The dogs make me forget about it and that makes me feel happy. Thank you and your dogs.

Love,

George

The dogs are part of the family at the House. They are invited to every event, every chapel service, every Mass—everything that happens at the House happens with a dog in attendance. Dogs have been there for visits from the Archbishop, baptisms, prayer services, weddings, and, sadly, memorial services. They have probably eaten everything that has been catered in for those events, because the kids won't let them go away hungry.

The dogs dress up on Halloween, accompanying the kids in their costumes. Angel once rode around the entire block in a toy car pedaled by Ashlynn without ever moving from the passenger seat. Teigh appeared at the House on Halloween as Batman and Superman and as Santa at Christmas.

The dogs are always invited to the annual volunteer appreciation dinner at the New York Athletic Club and recognized for their work. For their part in establishing the program, Teigh and Belle represented all of the therapy dogs and were honored on stage at the Waldorf Astoria, site of the annual Ronald McDonald House Gala that raises millions of dollars for the House every year.

If something is happening at or for the House, you can be certain that there will be therapy dog teams there, representing the program. This happens for a couple of reasons. First, the dogs can help set the mood and can help get families and kids to attend and be part of the event—having the dogs can be a draw for them. Once people are there, the dogs can help them relax and feel good about being there.

Second, the therapy dog teams are part of the House family—volunteers that are appreciated just as much as all of the other volunteers. I have always been impressed by how the staff treats and recognizes its volunteers. That's part of why there is a waiting list to volunteer there, and why volunteers stay for years.

The following statement is from the House's website (www.rmh-newyork.org):

> Ronald McDonald House of New York was created by volunteers and continues to rely on volunteers to enhance its services and programs. Your warm and caring presence as a volunteer has a positive impact on the life of a child and families who need to live at the House while undergoing cancer treatment at a local hospital.

• • • • • •

One summer Saturday night, Cheri and I had been out to dinner in the neighborhood with Teigh and Belle at a sidewalk café where the dogs could be part of the evening. While we were there, Cheri got a call to tell her that one of her kids had passed away at Morgan Stanley Children's Hospital. It was quite late, about 11 p.m., but we had to go by the House so she could make some calls and see what she could do to help the family.

We all walked into the empty lobby of the House. Cheri went back to her office, and I sat down in one of the lobby chairs with Teigh and Belle. We were the only ones in the lobby other than the night security guy, so we sat down and relaxed, waiting for Cheri to finish up.

Within about ten minutes, we had six young male residents—patients and siblings—join us in the lobby to hang out with Teigh and Belle. It was like some kind of phone chain had happened: "dogs in the House, pass it on."

There was not a parent in sight, and the kids technically are supposed to have an adult with them at all times, but it was a great moment. I took a picture of all of them with Teigh and Belle, and I called it "Bad Boys of the Ronald McDonald House." It reminded me of that public service ad: "It's 11 o'clock, do you know where your children are?"

It is a home away from home, after all.

• • • • • •

Remember the "pay attention" admonition from earlier in the book? I had a chance to find out what I was learning from the dogs with one of my kids at the House. A young girl named Eden was in town from California and had immediately checked into Memorial Sloan-Kettering for some tests. Cheri had met the family, and they had talked about dogs and the dog show together.

Eden asked Cheri to invite me to MSK to visit with her.

Eden was in the pediatrics unit at MSK, and dogs were not allowed there. Cheri assured me, "That's OK. They just want to talk about dogs. Bring some pictures, books, and a DVD, and they will keep you going for a while."

So off I went. I felt like I was missing something when I walked in the door—I kept looking down for the end of the leash. But we had a great visit, talking about Pugs for quite a while because Eden wanted to get one once she got healthy. I was there for over an hour with Eden and her mother, both of them sweethearts battling for Eden's survival.

I think that the visit worked out so well because I kept thinking, "What would Teigh and Belle do?" I thought about those wristbands that many people wear with "WWJD" printed on them, standing for "What Would Jesus Do?" Not to compare the dogs to Jesus, of course, but for this, my dogs were my inspiration.

I'm glad that I've been paying attention to them because it helped me help Eden.

Eventually, Eden got out of the hospital and came over to the House, where she got to spend up-close-and-personal time with Teigh and Belle.

· · · · · ·

In the moment.

I remind myself of this constantly. I know which children are facing the toughest battles at the time; I can see the difference in them physically from week to week. I have seen kids on a Tuesday night and attended their memorial services on Friday.

These are very special kids. They smile through un-imaginable pain. Their courage and their worldliness are amazing.

"How do you do it?" I hear this a lot. Not as much as Cheri hears it, but just about any time I share a story with someone about our visits. "Isn't it tough?"

Yes, it is tough. But it's not as tough on me as it is on the kids or the parents.

I am there for them with Teigh or Belle or Angel or Grace—there to provide some respite in their battle, there to lend some kind of normalcy to their frantic lives. But I am just the guy on the end of the leash. It's the dogs that are doing the work. If you ask Richard, who brings Tucker; Gay, who brings Mr. Gruffyd Babayan; Barbara, who brings Lille; Caroline, who brings Beau; Maria, who brings Ella; Nicole, who brings Lucy; Kris-tina, who brings Lilly; or any of the others, they will all give the same answer. We aren't doing it for ourselves.

I am biased, of course, but Ronald McDonald House is a wonderful place to be a volunteer. A wonderful, heart-warming, heartbreaking place, where doing something good for someone in need happens in the moment, one moment at a time.

CHAPTER 9

Champion Champions

In January of 1990, Westminster Kennel Club President Chet Collier asked me if I would be interested in doing the television commentary for the world's greatest dog show (my words) coming up in February. One of my Afghan Hounds was coming off a great year in the show ring, so I had met Chet on several occasions around the country at shows. He told me that they were looking for a new color commentator for the telecast, and someone had thrown my name into the mix because I had previously worked in PR for the Denver Broncos and the San Francisco 49ers as well as for ABC Sports as a publicist for *Monday Night Football*.

I had been in the right place at the right time—several times. I was working with the Broncos when they went to their first Super Bowl ever; I was working with the 49ers when they traded for O.J. Simpson; and *Monday Night Football* with Howard Cosell, Don Meredith, and Frank Gifford was already a huge part of the American sports culture when I started working with ABC Sports. I had been interviewed on camera a few times in those jobs, but I had never been a host or the "talent."

It really helped that I had been around the media madness that had surrounded the Broncos, O.J., and the *Monday Night* guys, and while all of that was not quite the same as standing in front of the camera, I accepted Chet's invitation to audition for Westminster. I was living in Seattle at the time, so he flew me to Boston, where he had a television production company. We did an audition tape with Chet playing the host to my color commentator, and we did our make-believe commentary over the tape of the Hound Group from the previous year's Westminster show.

He called the next day and offered me the job. I remember thinking to myself that this might be fun and that maybe I could make it last a couple of years.

Chet was the genius behind the television success of Westminster, thanks to his understanding of the world of television and the world of dog shows. Over the next few weeks, Chet and I talked about the show. I wanted his perspective, of course, and I felt the pressure of representing Westminster and our world of purebred dogs and dog shows to the general public, as Westminster was the show that everyone watched. I wanted Chet to be happy with my approach and my work.

Chet would often say, "It's important to remember that 99 percent of our television audience has never been to a dog show and probably will never go to a dog show." He also was resolute about Westminster's role in promoting and protecting the purebred dog in particular and responsible dog ownership in general, and why not? Westminster Kennel Club is, after all, the oldest organization in America dedicated to the sport of purebred dogs.

So with Chet's guidance, I made it my objective to talk about the real dogs and real people in our great family sport of showing dogs. It was important for the credibility of our messages that people understood that the same dogs they were seeing in the show ring are beloved family pets. These dogs don't spend their days between shows sitting around on doggy cushions eating doggy bonbons; they are real dogs that chew up our shoes, sleep on our couches, bark at the mailman, steal food off our counters, and shed on our clothes. I wanted everyone to realize that Westminster is a celebration of the world's greatest show dogs, but it is also a celebration of the dogs in our lives.

I gave all of the owners of the Best of Breed winners a TV information card to fill out so I would have something interesting to say about them on the telecast when they appeared in their Groups that evening. I asked them to tell me about more than their dogs' twenty-seven Group wins and nine Bests in Show; I asked them to tell me stories about what their dogs do at home or elsewhere.

I've gotten a lot of great stories on these cards over the years in a lot of categories:

Funny:
- A dog's favorite thing to do each day was to go through the drive-through at Dunkin' Donuts for donut holes
- A dog named Rembrandt was one of a litter of five, all named for toothpastes by their retired dentist owner
- A Dachshund accompanied his famous archaeologist owner on excavations; she said that he was an excellent digger but never kept notes and tended to mix up the bones

Near-tragic:
- One winner survived ingesting 176 allergy pills
- Another survived an airline mishap in which two of his littermates were killed
- Another winner survived being "misplaced" by the airline for eight hours en route to New York
- Others survived vehicle rollovers and crashes, emergency surgeries, and getting hit by a car

Please say "hi" to:
- Wives at home expecting to give birth any day
- The parishioners of an owner-handler who is a priest and knew he would have to answer to them for missing Mass on the Sunday before Westminster
- A handler's two daughters, who were both in the hospital about to deliver new grandchildren for her

Congratulations:
- To a handler, a mother of eight, who had just graduated from college. My question: "She had time to study?"

Hero awards (all dogs who won their Breeds at Westminster):
- To the dog who absorbed a shotgun blast and saved his owner's son
- To the dog who foiled an attempted armed robbery at his owner's veterinary clinic
- To the dog who saved his handler's husband from a house fire

I also found out how some of the winning dogs spent their time when not in the show ring. They had been part of print and television ad campaigns, in magazine articles (even as a "centerfold"), in MTV music videos, on Animal Planet's *Breed All About It*, in plays and operas, on *Hollywood Squares*, in movies, on *Oprah*, on the *Today Show*—and the list goes on.

Eventually, people began sharing stories about their dogs visiting children in schools, seniors in nursing homes, and patients in health care facilities. When these stories were told on television, they begat more stories. I wondered if the dogs had been doing these things all along, or if some of the owners heard that such stories made for good TV and subsequently got their dogs involved in these kinds of activities. However it happened, having a non-dog-show story about your show dog suddenly became a big deal, and people loved sharing those stories. Even better, therapy dogs started showing up everywhere. Even in the Best in Show ring.

The winners of Best in Show at the Westminster Kennel Club Dog Show instantly become the world's newest single-name celebrities. That gets confirmed many times on the day after the show with appearances on NBC's *Today Show*, CBS's *Early Show*, ABC's *Good Morning America*, and many other programs. There are photo opportunities at the Empire State Building, at Sardi's, and with Donald Trump. People holler at the dog ("Rufus, you can come to work with us any time," yelled a hard-hat construction worker in 2006); they come running over to take cell-phone pictures or call friends and family ("Mom, you'll never guess who I am standing with!"); they cheer as the dog passes by.

As great as they were as show dogs, some of the Westminster Best in Show winners had an even greater impact as therapy dogs. Some of them were officially registered and making regular visits. Others got a paw in the door due to their celebrity status and performed admirably in limited exposure. After all, show dogs are accustomed to strangers (judges and others) putting their hands on them and working in close quarters, and sometimes that makes the transition to being a therapy dog a little easier than it might be for non-show dogs.

In 2006, the Colored Bull Terrier Ch. Rocky Top's Sundance Kid capped a great show career by going Best in Show at Westminster. "Rufus" had previously won many Bests, but notably he captured BIS at two big shows in the fall of 2005—the Morris & Essex Dog Show and the National Dog Show presented by Purina—in a career that saw him become the top-winning Bull Terrier of all time.

Rufus became the hardest working dog in show business over the next few years, serving as a Therapy Dog Ambassador for the National Dog Show on NBC, doing appearances for Angel On A Leash, winning an American Kennel Club ACE (Award for Canine Excellence) in the therapy dog category, and helping to raise money for Bull Terrier rescue. All of this was in addition to his volunteer work with his just-as-hardworking owners, Barbara and Tom Bishop, visiting children's hospitals, schools, wounded soldiers at Walter Reed Army Medical Center, and many other people and places.

Rufus has his own Facebook page, on which his education is listed as follows: "Studied Therapy Dog at Westminster Kennel Club School of Best in Show Winners."

I was doing an interview once about Rufus, and I was asked if Rufus was in a class by himself because of all of the therapy dog work that he was doing. I gave the writer a great quote from Houston Oilers football coach Bum Phillips when he had been asked years ago about his star running back, Earl Campbell: "I don't know if he's in a class by himself, but whatever class he's in, it doesn't take long to take roll."

In this case, I told the interviewer, I know that Rufus and James are both sitting in the front row of that class.

James (Ch. Felicity's Diamond Jim), an English Springer Spaniel, had won top honors at Westminster in 2007 after a great career in which he had won nearly everything there was to win, including BIS at the AKC/ Eukanuba Invitational Championship. He was Number Two All-Breeds in 2006 and finished with fifty-one career Bests.

James was co-bred and co-owned by Terry Patton, with whom he lived. Terry is a dog trainer, and she volunteered with James in health care and extended care facilities. James began making nursing home visits when he was eight months old, and he eventually became an assistance dog and an emotional support dog for Terry's father, who suffered from dementia. "He was having a great career as a show dog, but he was unique in that regard because showing was not the most important thing in his world, or in ours," Terry said.

Along the way, James became a registered therapy dog, specializing in working with Alzheimer patients. Three days after his Westminster win, he visited one of his favorite senior care facilities in Fairfax, Virginia, where he had been a regular before his show career took him on the road. There, he celebrated with the residents, who served him dinner on a silver platter in honor of his win.

James made appearances all over the Washington, DC, area, helping to raise money for and awareness of Alzheimer's disease. He was the only canine celebrity in a star-studded group (including David Hyde Pierce and Dick Van Dyke) that helped launch the first Alzheimer's Association awareness campaign. He also made a number of appearances for Angel On A Leash to bring attention to the great work that therapy dogs do.

I watched James work many times, and I have always said that I thought he was the greatest working therapy dog I had ever seen. Every time I saw James working, he was focused on the person he was visiting, he was gentle and quiet, and he was totally responsive to Terry's nudges and commands at the same time. There aren't very many dogs who can do that; too many are very dependent on having direction to do what they do.

James came to Ronald McDonald House New York a number of times, and to watch him work was a thing of beauty. There are hundreds of pictures of therapy dogs at work at the House, and it's no surprise to me that James is in so many of them. He was a walking therapy dog textbook. Look up *therapy dog* in an encyclopedia, and there should be a picture of James; in fact, the Wikipedia entry used to feature a photo of him from one of his visits to the House. The kids and the parents were all fascinated with James—his attentive, gentle manner and consoling eyes. He was just the best.

Sadly, James passed in May of 2011, just before his eleventh birthday, losing a short battle to cancer. "He always gave 200 percent of himself, and had an indomitable spirit and a heart as big as the crowds that loved him," wrote Terry. "The bitter irony is that he delighted in visiting children who suffered from the same insidious disease that has now cut his life short as well."

James left huge pawprints to fill—show dog, therapy dog, service dog, beloved family dog. We will never see the likes of him again.

Among our other Best in Show winners, the Bichon Frise Ch. Special Times Just Right ("JR") from 2001 and the Sussex Spaniel Ch. Clussexx Three D Grinchy Glee ("Stump") from 2009 have made some therapy dog appearances as well, visiting pediatric patients at the famed M.D. Anderson Cancer Center in their hometown of Houston. Both dogs are co-owned by Scott Sommer and Cecelia Ruggles.

In 2011, Ch. Foxcliffe Hickory Wind ("Hickory"), the Scottish Deerhound, made a quick stop at Ronald McDonald House New York on the day after her Westminster Best in Show win. Early in the day, we had run into Archbishop Timothy Dolan in the green room at *Fox & Friends*; he was following us on the show. I had met him a few times at House activities, so I was not reluctant at all to ask him to bless Hickory. He did, referencing St. Francis and holding her head in his hands. That probably gave her some special strength for the day and some inspiration, perhaps, for her visit to the House later.

At the House, her imposing size and her quiet elegance made her a unique thought-provoking consideration for the kids and their families, and she drew a crowd in the lobby. Children circled her and stared, reaching out to touch her unique coat and face. Hickory's owner, Cecelia Dove, and handler, Angela Lloyd, were quite taken with the impact that Hickory made on the kids and the impact that the entire experience had on themselves.

Josh (Ch. Darbydale's All Rise Pouch Cove), the indomitable Newfoundland who captured Best in Show in 2004, went from show dog to therapy dog quite quickly, visiting extended-care patients on what seemed to be the weekend following his win. How can you not like a big fuzzy Newfoundland?

And then there's Uno. In 2008, Westminster's most famous winner in history used his celebrity to open a lot of doors for therapy dogs. The incomparable 15-inch Beagle, Ch. K-Run's Park Me In First, captured the hearts of people everywhere as he became the world's second-most-famous Beagle, behind only Snoopy. Remember that class I mentioned with Rufus and James? Uno is at the front of the line, standing at the door. We went through Delta Society therapy dog training with Michele Siegel. She loved him, and Uno was registered with me as his handler. He gets a lot done with his celebrity and his Beagle cuteness, but he is also "official," and that does so much for the credibility of therapy dogs everywhere.

Uno has been invited to events all over the country, and wherever he goes, he spreads a little joy. Caroline Dowell, Uno's owner, lived in Austin, Texas, and asked me if I would do most of the traveling with him. He was a great little dog who fit right in with my family. All of my dogs loved him, which is a good thing in a one-bedroom apartment in a Manhattan high-rise. Uno would come and live with us for a few weeks at a time, depending upon his media schedule.

The White House called, and Uno became the first Westminster winner ever to visit there, meeting President Bush and helping the First Lady put on a program for schoolchildren in the East Room. After the White House, Uno and his entourage visited some of our wounded warriors at Walter Reed Army Medical Center; it was a very special visit for all.

At Walter Reed, Uno formed a special bond with Lance Corporal Joshua Bleill, a Marine who had lost both of his legs in military action in Iraq. Lance Corporal Bleill was then invited to the 2009 Westminster show as a guest of the club. The day before the show, he and Uno went to Ronald McDonald House New York and visited with the pediatric oncology patients; some of them, like Josh, had amputated limbs. The next night, at the show, Josh and Uno were introduced on the floor of the Garden and received a rousing standing ovation.

Snoopy was Uno's best buddy, and Uno became the first Westminster winner to ride on a float in the Macy's Thanksgiving Day Parade when he was invited to be on the *Peanuts* (Universal Syndicate) float. Uno returned the favor by inviting Snoopy to come to the 2009 Westminster poster unveiling at Morgan Stanley Children's Hospital. Earlier, Uno had traveled to California to visit the Charles M. Schulz Museum and Knotts Berry Farm with Snoopy.

Uno walked the VIP red carpet with Hollywood celebrities at Matthew Perry's Lilly Clair Foundation charity event. He was recognized and mobbed at a street fair in Santa Monica the night before the event, but he still had the energy to visit kids at Ronald McDonald House in Los Angeles the next afternoon.

Uno and I had some great travel adventures in the summer of 2008. At the time, Midwest Airlines' Celebrity Pet Program allowed Uno to fly on a seat in the cabin (we had to purchase a ticket for him). He was always being recognized in airports, but we were often stopped by security personnel who wondered what a dog was doing walking around on the concourse. After a while, they knew who he was, especially at LaGuardia (New York), Mitchell (Milwaukee), and Dallas/Fort Worth airports. He stayed in the best hotels and was welcomed in the best restaurants wherever he went.

I learned how to use every cell-phone camera ever made, as people would come up to us, hand me their cell phones, and ask, "Will you take our picture with Uno?" Oprah's *O Magazine* ran a story written by Oprah's life coach, who talked about how everyone should strive to create Uno's "It Factor" for themselves.

Uno traveled with his own printed airline ticket, just like any other passenger. It read "Uno Frei" whenever he was traveling with me. And like any other air traveler, he was subject to security considerations. At the security checkpoint in St. Louis, we were going through, with Uno in my arms as usual, and the security personnel took a look at his boarding pass. On it was the code to indicate that the computer had selected this passenger to undergo additional screening.

The TSA folks, who rarely exhibited a sense of humor about anything, had to smile at this one. But they still pulled us out of line and took Uno over to the screening area, where they proceeded to wand him and pat him down (he wasn't wearing a coat or anything). They did seem to see the humor in this and were taking pictures the whole time. When they were done, I said, "It's good to be able to tell everyone that the world is safe from terrorist Beagles." And I actually saw a few of them smile.

That ticket is still on the wall in my office.

Uno was a member of the Midwest mileage program and was welcomed in all of their "Care Clubs" in terminals around the country. All of this came to an end when Midwest was purchased by Republic Airlines and the Premier Pet Program was discontinued, but it was a great run.

Uno visited Ronald McDonald House New York a number of times, including one celebrity-rich evening with James. He visited children and seniors at Hackensack University Medical Center in New Jersey, where they have a great Angel program. He also visited kids in Ronald McDonald Houses in St. Louis, Los Angeles, and Milwaukee.

He was invited to throw out the first pitch for major league baseball games in Milwaukee and St. Louis. The highlight of his trip to Milwaukee, and perhaps of his therapy dog career—so far—was his visit to Ronald McDonald House in Milwaukee, which was affiliated with Children's Hospital. I had asked my friend Bill Sullivan, CEO of Ronald McDonald House New York, for a contact name so I could see about bringing Uno to the House in Milwaukee. Bill lined me up with executive director Pam Buckley, and I called her to ask if I could bring Uno by for a visit with the kids and families. She said sure, and we blocked out the afternoon before the evening baseball game.

I invited Maggie Butterfield and others from Volunteer Services at the hospital to come along. They have a great therapy dog program and were becoming an Angel On A Leash facility, so I thought that they should be a part of this.

When we walked in the door at the House, we found several kids and families waiting for us. I also saw a number of adults hanging around the front room who didn't seem to be with any of the kids. I had been visiting Ronald McDonald House New York for three years by this time, so I could tell the difference between family and "purpose-driven" spectators.

Pam pulled me and Uno aside. "I had a nice conversation with Bill Sullivan, and he couldn't say enough good things about Uno and you," she said, "but I have a confession to make here. We don't allow dogs in the House, we are making an exception for Uno.

"All of these people that you see hanging out are members of our board. The board has turned down proposals for therapy dog programs in the past, but we invited them to come and meet Uno. We are hopeful that if Uno puts on a good therapy dog show for them, we will be able to renew the conversation with the board about allowing therapy dogs in here on a regular basis. Not to put any pressure on you ..."

"We'll make it happen for you; thanks for the advance notice," I told her, with a wink. "Subtly show me the big hitters on the board, and we'll make sure they get their money's worth."

So Uno and I had a little something extra riding on this visit. He and I had been visiting many places as a therapy dog team, but, admittedly, it was occasionally based more on Uno's celebrity than his therapy dog training. But he had been through the therapy dog class with me, we had passed, and I handle him exactly the way that I handle any of my own therapy dogs. He was pretty responsive—a little rough around the edges, but he had just turned three years old at this point and was learning with each visit we made. He had already touched a lot of people as a therapy dog. None of this really mattered to the folks in the Milwaukee House, but it gave me a little confidence as I thought about playing for a big prize.

Well, we had a great visit. Uno was perfect—wagging his tail, engaging the kids, giving a "*rooooo*" when I asked for it, accepting pets and hugs, posing for pictures. The kids were responsive, and the parents loved it. I could not have drawn it up any better than it actually happened, and it must have been good, because I was really worn out when the visit was over.

That done, we headed to the ball game. We had invited kids and families from the Children's Hospital of Wisconsin to the stadium to be guests in Uno's VIP suite, where he entertained them throughout the evening.

Uno was a star that night, too. He visited the Brewers' clubhouse, posed for pictures for charity, threw out the first pitch with Milwaukee pitcher Jeff Suppan, danced on the dugout roof during the seventh-inning stretch, was a gracious host in his private suite, and did everything you could ask of a celebrity without any of the drama. After the game, both of us exhausted, Uno and I celebrated quietly, eating dinner with our friends from the hospital and from Ronald McDonald House at a sidewalk restaurant outside our hotel. I don't remember the score of the baseball game, but I couldn't help but feel like we had indeed won something that day.

A few months later, Pam called me to report that the board had approved a therapy dog program for Milwaukee's Ronald McDonald House. "Thank you for making it happen," she said, "and thank Uno for us, too."

66 *We knew that there were going to be lots of friends—four-legged and two-legged— waiting in Heaven to greet her.* **99**

CHAPTER 10

Making Rounds

It was my normal Monday night of visiting in the women's health unit at Sloan-Kettering.

"Hey, I know you," said the woman, looking up from her bed as Angel and I entered her room.

"Well, of course you do," I said. "This is Angel, my Cavalier. You've seen her on the MSK therapy dog calendar. She's Miss May."

"No, I mean I know you," she said.

"Well, I have been visiting up here for nearly three years now; have you been here before?"

"No, I watch you on TV every year. You're the Westminster guy, David Frei."

"Are you a dog show person?" I asked.

"No, but I love the show and I love you; you're so good at it," she said.

"Well, I'm flattered. Thanks for watching. Lots of people work hard to make it a good show."

"And you do that show on Thanksgiving Day, too, with Mr. Peterman."

"Yes, the National Dog Show."

"I watch that one, too. You're great."

"Now you're embarrassing me; thanks. I couldn't do it without John O'Hurley. I think we're a pretty good team."

"You are, but now I am really mad," she said.

"Mad at us?"

"No, I'm mad because I had to get cancer to meet David Frei."

"OK, well now you've done both. Let's work on the cancer part of it, let's think good thoughts, and let's get you on your way home."

· · · · · ·

I used to visit NewYork-Presbyterian/Weill Cornell's cardiac unit when Cheri was doing her residency there. The routine was to come to the nurses' station and ask who needed a visit. Sometimes the nurses had a list ready; sometimes they were winging it. In the latter case, we would get started with a couple of their suggestions and then check back as they thought about it some more.

So on this particular night, Teigh and I were working the floor diligently. One of the nurses came to me and said, "We'd like you to try Mr. Johnson in 402B. A visit might do him some good."

"OK, we're off."

We went to the room, a double room, and my target patient was in the bed on the far side of the room. A woman I presumed to be his wife was sitting in a chair bedside. I stood in the doorway and said from across the room, "Hi, Mr. Johnson. Is this a good time for a visit from Teigh, my therapy dog?"

He looked at me and said something to his wife, who got up and came over to us. "Not only does he not want a visit, he's not happy that you are even in here."

My response was different than what I was actually thinking. "Sorry to bother him. Have a nice evening."

We get rejected occasionally when someone isn't feeling well, or is falling asleep, or has other visitors, but this was the first time that I had gotten a slapdown with a rejection.

I headed right back to the nurses' station. "Hey, what's the story with Mr. Johnson? He just chased us out; rather, his wife chased us out, somewhat irritated. Did I get the room number wrong?"

Two nurses, ones that I worked with every week, looked at one another with weak smiles.

"We're sorry," one of them said. "This guy has been a total jerk here for the past couple of days, and his wife isn't much better. They have a problem with everything we do. They're making everyone's lives miserable. We just were trying to find something that he might respond to. We hope you're not too upset with us for throwing you in there; we probably should have warned you."

"Is it an issue of patient confidentiality when a guy is a jerk?" I winked. "I can take it; I've had badder guys than that in my face. I just hope that he didn't hurt Teigh's feelings."

• • • • • •

When Cheri was at New York-Presbyterian, she came to know a patient on the bone marrow transplant unit (BMT). The patient, Julie, was a wonderful woman whose body had already rejected two transplants, and she was not doing well.

She missed her own dog, had a history of working with dogs in need, and had some involvement in the dog show world with her own dog, an English Foxhound. She was able to convince her health care team to allow Teigh and Belle to visit her, something that had never been allowed before on the BMT at NewYork-Presbyterian. She had also asked that Cheri bring me along to talk about dogs and Westminster.

The rooms on the BMT are set up to keep out any possible pathogens—double doors, negative airflow, scrub sinks, and other precautionary measures. Visitors have to scrub in at a sink between the two doors and put on masks, gowns, and gloves before they enter.

We do all of those things ourselves and put a little hand sanitizer on the bottom of the dog's feet as another precaution; the patient puts on a gown, mask, and gloves for the visit from the dog. When we go in to see the patient, we put the dog in a chair next to the bed, where the patient can interact by petting or just looking at the dog.

The masks can't hide the patients' smiles.

We didn't know Julie long, but we quickly realized that she was quite special. We learned from her husband, Tim, that she had a successful career in the music industry and then created a company that helped transition traumatic brain-injury patients in New York City back into their communities and jobs.

We learned about Julie's beloved English Foxhound, Anna, who inspired Julie to extend her grace and caring into the animal world. While Julie did a lot for Anna, it was what Anna did for her that motivated Julie to spend her spare time in New York finding homes for homeless dogs and to buy bags of food to feed stray dogs wherever she traveled on vacation.

We had some wonderful visits with Julie before she passed. She would have been pleased to learn that Teigh and Belle also attended her church memorial service at St. Anthony's in New York. Their rattling dog tags got everyone to turn around and smile as they walked in.

Julie's legacy was opening doors everywhere for society's marginalized people and dogs. We knew that there were going to be lots of friends—four-legged and two-legged—waiting in Heaven to greet her. We were blessed to have had Julie touch our lives, no matter how briefly. She really does live on in all of us.

• • • • • •

Kathleen was another BMT patient. She asked Cheri to bring Teigh and Belle to her, and the doctors approved. Cheri brought me along on the visits a number of times.

After Kathleen passed, the family asked that we bring the dogs to the memorial service, and we did. After the service, we went downstairs to the reception with the dogs and promptly drew a crowd.

"Is this Teigh and Belle?" one of Kathleen's friends asked. "Having the dogs visit meant so much to her."

"We were glad that we could help bring her some peace at the end," Cheri answered.

Another woman joined the group. "She loved the dogs," she said, "but I have to tell you this story. I came to visit Kathleen one day, and I go through the first door and stop to 'scrub in.' I wash up, I put on booties, a gown, gloves, a mask, and a hat, ready to visit. I back through the door, careful not to touch anything, and I turn around to see her and ... THERE'S A DOG IN THE ROOM!"

We all laughed, understanding how someone could be surprised by that.

"She loved these dogs," the woman said, through tears. "Thanks for bringing them to her, and thanks for bringing them here today so we could thank them ourselves."

• • • • • •

Teigh and I were part of a video shoot at Morgan Stanley Children's Hospital one day, and afterward we visited a few patients. One of them was a young boy named Adam—a bright, worldly little guy. Cheri has often told me that her pediatric patients are wise old souls for all that they have been through, and that indeed was Adam.

I put Teigh into Adam's bed, laying him along Adam's side. His mom was telling me Adam's story.

"He's had seventeen surgeries in two years," she said, almost in a daze.

"I'm a brave little boy," Adam said.

No kidding, Adam. We should all have your courage.

• • • • • •

One of the things that I do that has had the most impact on me in recent years began with having nothing to do with dogs ... well, *almost* nothing (as if anything in my life can have nothing to do with dogs!).

My friend Linda Woo called me in Seattle in 2000 and asked if I would do her a favor. She was going to receive an honor from Transfiguration Church and School in Manhattan's Chinatown, and she wanted me to come to New York City and serve as the master of ceremonies at their fund-raising dinner-dance.

I accepted the invitation, of course. Linda has been a wonderful friend through the years. I met her through my friend Wayne Ferguson. She told me that the event was to be held at a restaurant in Chinatown, where Transfiguration has been an active Catholic community since 1801. They added a free school for immigrant children in 1832, and it has been serving Lower Manhattan ever since. In fact, Linda graduated from the school, became Miss Chinatown, and has been an active supporter of their Transfiguration Education Association (TEA) ever since.

While the school served the neighborhood's German and Italian immigrant residents for many years, today it is in the heart of what has become Chinatown, and most of the students are of Chinese heritage. The school has been filled to its 260-student capacity with an active waiting list for the past twenty-five years. It features a challenging curriculum that comes from the state and from the Archdiocese of New York.

It is, as I have come to know and appreciate, a very special place. The man who makes it all happen is Father Ray Nobiletti, pastor of the church and overseer of the school. Dr. Patrick Taharally is principal of Transfiguration School, and Emily Eng-Tran is principal of the Kindergarten School. I am constantly impressed with their work and their wonderful students. They have all become special friends, and Father Ray, the heart and soul of it all, has become a mentor for Cherilyn, too.

The dinner-dance event is held in a huge restaurant with nearly 1,000 guests in attendance. I have to admit that when Linda first described it to me as a dinner at a restaurant, I figured that there would be a couple of hundred people—but nothing like this.

At this annual event, the TEA has honored people and companies who have contributed to the school, to the community, and to the revitalization of Lower Manhattan (Transfiguration is only a few blocks from Ground Zero). Among those who have been recognized through the years are State Supreme Court Justice Michael Corriero, John Cardinal O'Connor, journalist Pete Hamill, actor Robert DeNiro, photographer Corky Lee, businessman Ben Glascoe, businesswoman Amy Mak Chan, educator Regina Mah-Yee, City Council Speaker Christine Quinn, New York City Schools Chancellor Joel Klein, educator Dr. Nancy Eng, educators A.B. Whitfield and Janey Whitney, and the Lower Manhattan Development Corporation.

I was humbled to be one of the 2006 TEA honorees. My award was artwork done by one of the students, inscribed as follows:

David Frei
Humanitarian, Communications and
Broadcast Professional
Honoring his loyal support of
Transfiguration Schools
and his dedication to philanthropic causes

In the past, we had taken Teigh and Belle to the Transfiguration kindergarten, where they were big hits. The TEA probably should have honored the dogs instead of me, because they generated more smiles and excitement than you could imagine.

Teigh and Belle captivated the kids. Judging from their questions and the way they acted around the dogs, I guessed that not many of the kids lived in households with their own dogs, so meeting and interacting with Teigh and Belle was a new experience for most of them. Teigh and Belle ate it up, of course, holding court, accepting pets and hugs, and performing a few tricks as Cheri and I talked about dogs in our lives and responsible dog ownership.

The kids at Transfiguration are wonderfully unrelenting and talented. My guess is that they learn these qualities and hone their talents at this great school, which is why they consistently perform above grade level in standardized state tests.

I am so blessed to have Transfiguration and people like Father Ray in my life.

• • • • • •

In a lot of things that I do in the media and in public, it's important for me to know my audience. That's important for handlers in therapy dog work, too, especially for the safety of the dogs.

After her residency at NewYork-Presbyterian, Cheri was offered the position of director of the Department of Spiritual Care at Terence Cardinal Cooke (TCC) Health Care Center, a big hospital on Fifth Avenue near the north end of Central Park in East Harlem.

TCC is a 700-bed hospital that has a number of special-care units, and two of them require our full attention when visiting: the Huntington's disease and AIDS units.

Huntington's disease is a genetic neurodegenerative brain disease that presents with sudden mood swings, irritability, and fits of anger, along with *chorea*, which is a term for sudden or jerky movements. The Huntington's unit at TCC is the best of its kind in the country. The patients there loved the dogs, but the challenge was always to protect the dogs from anything that comes with the symptoms of the disease. Often, we would have to gently encourage patients to loosen their grips on Teigh or Belle, who were remarkably tolerant and did a lot of good on their visits to this unit.

We had begun our therapy dog career visiting at an AIDS hospice in Seattle, so I thought I knew what to expect in TCC's long-term care unit. What was new to me as a volunteer and also to Cheri was the fact that a number of these patients had been violent criminals and aggressive street people. It was difficult and not particularly wise for Cheri to visit on her own, and she usually took Ron, a 350-pound Detroit-cop-turned-Catholic-priest with her. Occasionally, I would go with her. One night I got the question, "Hey, where's the big guy?" I answered, "I'm the biggest guy you're going to get today."

The dog's nature is to trust everyone, so the lesson falls to you, the dog's handler: protect your dog at all times. As the handler and as the dog's advocate, it is your responsibility to know who you are visiting and always be prepared.

• • • • • •

I know that the people we visit appreciate our work, but they don't get the chance to do much other than throw us a quick thank-you as we walk out the door. And that's fine; we know that they do appreciate us, and we understand the circumstances. But to run into some thank-yous later can be pretty special.

We were at Saks Fifth Avenue for the Angel On A Leash charity event with Uno in 2009 when two ladies approached me. They looked like well-to-do Saks customers, like all of those who were there, having their pictures taken with Uno.

"Hi, David. I know that you probably don't remember us," one of them began, introducing herself, "but you and your dog Belle visited our mother at Sloan-Kettering last fall, and we were there in the room with her. We met you then. We saw that you were going to be here, and we wanted to come by and thank you again."

That was nice. "I'll let Belle know that you were here. That's great that you would come to find me. Please give my best to your mother."

"She sends her best, too," the daughter said, "and asked us to tell you to give Belle a hug for her."

"Well, I can certainly make that happen. Tell her that Belle sends her love!"

Occasionally I will see someone on his or her repeat visit to Sloan-Kettering. One night, I walked into a room with Grace, and the patient jumped out of bed with excitement.

"Oh, I am so excited that you are here," she said. "I have saved this picture of Angel ever since my last time here, a few months ago, when she came to see me."

With that, she showed me a picture of Angel and her in her hospital bed from that visit.

"I want to get a picture of Grace and me to add to the collection," she said, handing her cell phone to her visiting friend to take a photo. "Here, put Grace right here," she said, patting the bed.

"That's great," I said. "We're always good for a picture for you."

Another evening, we were sitting at Finnegan's with Teigh and Belle, and we struck up a conversation with a couple sitting at the table next to us. They asked about the dogs, and eventually the conversation came around to the work that they did at Sloan-Kettering and Ronald McDonald House.

The ladies at the table on the other side of us, who couldn't help but hear our conversation, were getting up to leave and stopped to pet Teigh and Belle.

"Actually, I know all about you and Belle," said one of them.

"How is that?" I asked.

"Personal experience. I was a patient, and you came to visit me," she said. "It was such a great visit; you took my mind off my pain and my feeling sorry for myself. I thought about you often and always wished I had thanked you more."

That made me smile. "Just seeing you sitting here and the fact that you are out and about is about as huge a thank-you as you can give me."

Teigh and Belle.

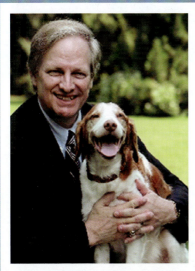

The "you really do start to look like your dog as you get older" picture.

Belle, a.k.a. Ch. Hope's Know-Belle Award JH.

David and Cherilyn at an Angel benefit.

Belle and a friend at Ronald McDonald House.

Cherilyn, Belle, and Teigh.

Belle and Teigh romp at Cannon Beach, Oregon.

The "Bad Boys of Ronald McDonald House" on a Saturday night.

Karen Pelletier was our first patient at
Memorial Sloan-Kettering Cancer Center.

House resident Eden
leans on Teigh and Belle.

Teigh and Belle bring lots
of smiles.

Teigh creates a moment for a senior citizen in extended care.

Belle at Morgan Stanley Children's Hospital.

George wrote a wonderful letter about what the dogs mean to him.

A little love changes everything.

A sketch by Brian Narelle, an audience member at one of David's presentations.

Grace and Angel get their turn in a studio shot.

Puppy Grace with her friend Chloe at the Ronald McDonald House block party.

Angel was a huge hit in her surgical scrubs, posing for the Sloan-Kettering therapy dog calendar.

Angel shares her love with Deyja at the Ronald McDonald House block party.

Angel makes a new friend at the block party.

First graders smile for Angel at a school visit.

Angel and our buddy, the valiant Jessie Kuebler.

Finnegans Wake

Like Teigh and Belle did, Grace and Angel know that good things happen at our Upper East Side hangout.

Angel and Cherilyn visit with a young House resident.

Ashlynn gave Grace a ride around the Ronald McDonald House block in her Barbie car.

Angel goes a lot of places in her Sherpa bag.

Angel entertained Uno whenever he came to visit us; here they are at the Westminster office.

Emmy and Grace hanging out at the House.

David (RIGHT) with dear friend Karen LeFrak, a great supporter of of therapy dog work and Angel On A Leash, and AKC president Dennis Sprung.

Michele Siegel is the star Delta Society instructor and evaluator who has trained all four of David's dogs, plus Uno!

ABOVE: Mike Lingenfelter and his heroic service dog, Dakota, whose remarkable story was told in David's earlier book, *The Angel by My Side*, coauthored with Mike.

LEFT: "More dog!" Alain the Labrador with Tom Lasley and hospital professionals from Providence (Portland, Oregon).

Clayton visits with a young patient at Morgan Stanley Children's Hospital.

The Angel On A Leash logo.

Lille and Ben share some quiet time together.

Mr. Gruffyd Babayan helped keep his pal Joey active before a heart transplant.

The smile says it all!

A pediatric oncology patient is fascinated by Stump at M.D. Anderson Cancer Center in Houston.

The huge Josh was a huge hit at Morgan Stanley Children's Hospital after his Westminster win.

Westminster winner Hickory was popular at the House after her big win.

Rufus makes friends and brings smiles.

James gets the therapeutic touch from a young House resident.

American heroes at Walter Reed spend some time with Uno.

Uno made things happen at the Milwaukee House.

Three young heroes compare notes at the House.

Marine hero Josh Bleill joined Uno on a visit to the House.

Andrea and Uno at the House, where he was a regular visitor.

Uno and Laura at the House.

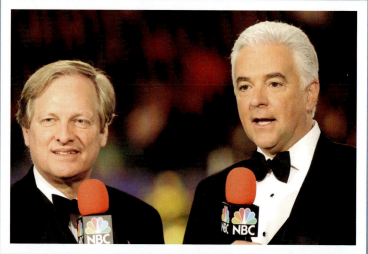

David and John O'Hurley have been the on-air cohosts of the National Dog Show presented by Purina on NBC since its inception in 2002.

Transfiguration Church and School is an important part of David's life.

Playing a dog show judge on Sex and the City wasn't too much of a reach for David; the win went to Charlotte (Kristin Davis) and her dog, Elizabeth Taylor.

David's dad, Jerry, was a P-38 photo recon pilot in the South Pacific during World War II.

David at about five years old on a fishing trip with Dad.

David's dad on the field as the Oregon football coach, shown here with one of his favorites, Ken Woody.

David's brother, Terry Frei; his dad, Jerry; and David in Eugene, Oregon, in the early 1990s for a reunion of Jerry's Oregon teams in his honor.

Artist Susan Bahary, David, and Bill Wynne.

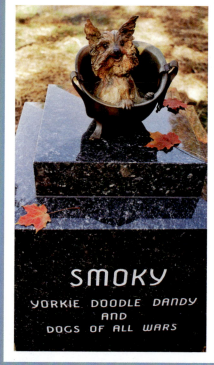

PHOTO COURTESY OF WILLIAM WYNNE

SMOKY

YORKIE DOODLE DANDY
AND
DOGS OF ALL WARS

PHOTO COURTESY OF WILLIAM WYNNE

War hero Smoky—"Yorkie Doodle Dandy."

The memorial in Cleveland Metroparks by Susan Bahary is one of six memorials nationwide.

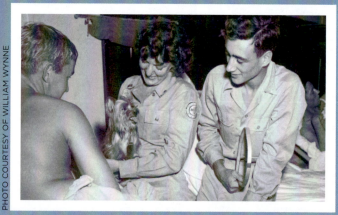

PHOTO COURTESY OF WILLIAM WYNNE

Smoky just may have been the first recognized therapy dog.

Family portrait: Belle, Teigh, and Angel (FRONT) with Cherilyn and David.

With three dogs in a one-bedroom Manhattan apartment, it's a good thing that they love each other!

Angel was especially protective of Teigh in his final days.

Grace and Angel at Teigh and Belle's gravesite.

David the dog walker on the streets of New York with Angel (LEFT), Uno (FRONT), Teigh (BACK), and Belle (RIGHT).

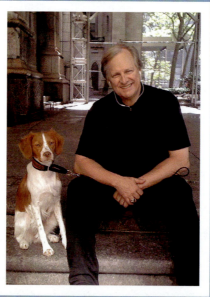

David and Grace one morning at St. Patrick's Cathedral in New York.

Elizabeth Taylor and Me

Occasionally, someone recognizes me in public from my television work ("Hey, you're the dog guy" or "Hey, Westminster!"). That's not a big deal to me, but it can be fun. I've been doing Westminster on TV since 1990, after all, and the National Dog Show since 2002. There are millions of people in the viewing audiences, so I hope that I come across some people out there who have seen the shows.

There was one time in particular when I was very pleasantly and genuinely surprised by the recognition. In late 2003, the people at *Sex and the City* asked me if I would be interested in playing a role in one of their final episodes. This was very exciting for me; I loved the show and had watched it from its beginning in 1998. As the series was coming to an end, the world was watching.

They wanted me for the role of a dog show judge, so it wasn't a huge stretch. I read for the role and answered their questions about how I thought the scene should play out so that it would be (mostly) technically correct from a dog show standpoint while still allowing for some creative license. I guess they liked what I had to offer, because I got the part. They also accepted my suggestion to use my friend Wayne Ferguson, president of the Kennel Club of Philadelphia/National Dog Show, to play the dog show PA announcer. I felt great about how they involved me, and I was excited to be a part of it.

We were scheduled to shoot the dog show, the so-called "Astor Classic," one evening on location in New York City at the world-famous Roseland Ballroom. They brought in a bunch of show dogs and handlers from the tri-state area, many of whom were friends of mine. The way everything was set up, the grooming area and the ring, I really did feel like I was at a dog show. Well, a small dog show, anyway.

I had my own little dressing room in one of the production trucks; that was a kick, and I was loving the whole experience. When my makeup call came, I headed for the makeup truck. It was a couple of hours before our scene was to be shot, but I imagined that they were getting us lesser players out of the way so they could make their four female stars even more beautiful.

They put me in a chair at the far end of the truck, probably where they put all the rookies. As they were working on me, I saw a few people come in and sit down, but I couldn't really tell who they were. I chatted with a man and a woman in the chairs next to me; they had been in the show in small roles before ("no small roles, only small actors"), and they told me how much they loved the crew and the stars in personal, stand-around-and-visit situations.

When they were through making me up, I got up to leave and had to walk behind all of the other chairs to get to the door. Just as I got to the door, I glanced to the left and saw Sarah Jessica Parker sitting there, looking back at me in the mirror. I smiled, and before I could say anything, she said, "Hey, I know who you are; you're the dog guy! I watch you on TV all the time!"

OK, take me now, God; I have everything I've ever needed in my life. I have been watching *Sex and the City* since its very first episode and considered myself a faithful fan, especially of Sarah Jessica, so to hear that from her, well ...

I laughed and replied, "Thanks. I watch you all the time, too, Sarah Jessica. I am a great fan. Thanks for having me here tonight." I spent the rest of the night thinking of all of the things I could have possibly said that would have been more witty and charming.

In the show, I was judging the Toy Group, which included Charlotte (played by Kristin Davis) and her Cavalier, named Elizabeth Taylor, competing against a number of my friends. And here's a surprise: Charlotte and Elizabeth Taylor were my winners. Admittedly, I hardly looked at her dog or any of the other dogs. That's the way it was written, and I didn't have any trouble following the script. Here is the way that the episode synopsis from HBO describes it: "Elizabeth takes first prize, largely due to the judge being sweet on Charlotte." My friend John Mandeville, the columnist for *Dog News*, used the word *lecherous* in his description, but I thought that was a little strong. Smitten ... that would be OK.

We shot the end of the scene the next night. I brought Belle to the shoot that second night, which brought me into a long conversation with Sarah Jessica, who told me that she grew up with a Brittany as her family dog and loved the breed. I was grateful to have this "do-over" from my previous night's meeting with Sarah Jessica in the makeup truck, and I thought that I was witty and charming this time. She was as gracious and elegant and beautiful in person as she is on television and in movies.

The episode ("The Cold War," episode #91) aired on February 1, 2004, and was one of the final episodes of the series. I had a couple of close-ups, and my name was in the credits for one of the hottest shows on television—and I got a paycheck. I could go through life like this. As a bonus, all these years later, I still get an occasional residual check for a couple of dollars each time the show airs somewhere, along with phone calls and emails from friends ("Hey, your *Sex and the City* episode is on right now"), which are nice reminders of the entire experience.

Kristin Davis was a sweetheart, too. We had a lot of "hurry-up-and-wait" time between takes of our scene, and I felt like I was hanging out with a friend. A couple of years later, in 2006, Kristin came to Westminster to plug the release of her new movie, *The Shaggy Dog*, and we had a little visit on the air, reminiscing about her dog show handling experience and my judging in *Sex and the City*.

The winners always like the judges, of course. And even though her win was scripted, I think Kristin was caught up in all of the Westminster hoopla and felt like she and Elizabeth Taylor had gotten a big win under me. She fit right in at Westminster.

CHAPTER 12

My Character-Rich World

I f I had a dollar for every time someone asks me about the movie *Best in Show*, I could retire and live on that income (along with my hefty residuals from *Sex and the City*, of course). Well, that may be a bit of an overstatement, especially since my residuals are down to about $2, but I could still get a lot of good dinners.

My stock answer is that I love *Best in Show*, I love the fact that the Westminster Kennel Club Dog Show is a big enough part of the American landscape that it could be the subject of this brilliant satire, and I love that *Best in Show* lives on and on, just like Westminster itself. This movie came out in 2000, and I still get asked about it every year when I go on the publicity circuits for both Westminster and the National Dog Show.

Yes, there are a lot of things in the movie that could well happen in the dog show world in which I live, where we have a character-rich environment. I tell everyone that I do in fact know many of the characters in the movie and that my wife has indeed yelled at me when our "Busy

Bee"-equivalent toy was not in the dog's show bag ("You go back and get her Busy Bee!").

The movie is as quote-rich as it is character-rich. I liked the yuppie couple the most, played by Parker Posey and Michael Hitchcock, and the talk of their meeting at Starbucks and the quote about being lucky to have been "raised amongst catalogs" were perfect. I still laugh when I think about Harlan Pepper's (Christopher Guest) nut-naming, Buck Laughlin's (Fred Willard) TV color commentary, just about anything from Gerry Fleck (Eugene Levy), and really anything else from the movie, for that matter. The advice given by one of Harlan's friends as Harlan and his Bloodhound set out for Philadelphia: "If you get tired, pull over; if you get hungry, eat something"—still gets quoted on any road trip I am a part of.

This movie is a big part of my life—not just because I walk around quoting the dialogue. It's because it brought about the creation of the National Dog Show on NBC.

It all began when Jon Miller watched the movie and found it to be hysterical. Jon is the creative genius who is now president of programming for NBC Sports and VERSUS sports network. He's the guy who came up with the hugely successful National Hockey League Winter Classic, the outdoor hockey game played on New Year's Day and broadcast on NBC. He oversees 8,000 hours of sports programming, including every big sporting event you can think of, from the Kentucky Derby to Wimbledon to Notre Dame football to the Dew Action Sports Tour and more.

He started thinking about how entertaining the dog show concept was and what he might be able to do with it. He found Wayne Ferguson, show chairman for the

Kennel Club of Philadelphia. Wayne is my best friend in dogs, so I am biased, but anyone can tell you that he is an astute businessman, too. He created Cherrybrook Pet Supplies years ago from the trunk of his car and built it into a multimillion-dollar operation.

So these two smart guys got together, and the concept was underway. Jon found a sponsor, Purina, and now all they had to do was to get the show on TV in a good time slot.

NBC had walked away from broadcasting NFL football games on Thanksgiving a few years prior and had been showing movies, such as *It's A Wonderful Life*, after the popular Macy's parade, but the movies weren't getting much in the way of ratings in spite of a handoff from the highly rated telecast of the parade. From a business standpoint, in spite of huge ratings, the telecast of the parade was not an advertising bonanza, as retailers were unable to purchase advertising for the parade telecast because it was a Macy's exclusive. Low-rated movies that followed were not the answer for advertisers.

So Jon took a swing for the fences, asking for the time slot following the parade. His NBC bosses bought into it. The National Dog Show presented by Purina was born. Wayne told Jon that he wanted me for the television commentary, and Jon liked that idea. I asked Chet Collier if he would approve of my doing the commentary for another dog show. Chet thought it would be a good way to promote the sport and that it would have great value for promoting the Westminster telecast as well, so he gave it his blessing.

At the same time, the NBC guys went directly to John O'Hurley (*Seinfeld*'s Mr. Peterman) to see if he would host the show. They had gotten to know John well from the American Century celebrity golf tournament in Lake Tahoe every summer and thought that he would be a good host. They landed him, which was a huge catch for the show.

Sears, Target, and Best Buy signed on. And for that first dog show on Thanksgiving Day in 2002, some 20 million viewers came along for the ride, staying tuned to NBC following the Macy's Thanksgiving Day Parade.

John and I had a great time, our numbers were huge, and everyone seemed happy. Not long after this, General Electric (which owned NBC) bought USA Network, bringing my two dog-show-carrying networks together. I couldn't have drawn it up any better.

John has been a great partner over the years. Thanksgiving 2011 will mark the tenth year of the show and our tenth year together. That's a long partnership; compare it with the Westminster telecast on USA, where I have had eight partners in twenty-two years (one of them, Joe Garagiola, for nine of those years). In spite of how that may sound, I'm really not that hard to work with!

John is an entertainer and is perfect for our two-hour, produced-for-television, family show. I'll be sitting there, and I swear that I hear Mr. Peterman speaking. I find myself laughing out loud at lines like these:

"A sheep has crashed the competition!" (Bedlington Terrier)

"Oh Whoopi, we found your hair!" (Puli)

"Here's one that we usually see at the other end of a Frisbee." (Border Collie)

"This dog looks like it incapacitates its quarry by saliva." (Bloodhound)

Besides that great wit, he is smart and always has good questions for me, asking what he knows would be of interest to the people watching at home. The greatest pressure he brings me is his status as one of the world's sexiest men (according to People magazine). He's tall (6'3"), has great hair and a great voice, and is a *Dancing with the Stars* champion. It's tough standing next to him; I'm always worrying what that makes me look like!

John is a star, and he's fun to be around because in spite of that star status, he doesn't take himself or the rest of the world too seriously. We have become great personal friends, too. Cheri and I have had a lot of wonderful times with John and his wife, Lisa, and that helps our partnership in the telecast. We have stayed with them in Las Vegas to watch him perform in *Spamalot*, and we have seen him in *Chicago* on Broadway. Cheri arranged for her colleague and our friend Monsignor Thomas Modugno of St. Monica Parish in New York City to baptize their son, William.

When John was writing his first book, *It's Okay to Miss the Bed on the First Jump* (2006), he wanted to include something about therapy dog work. I lined him up with Greer Griffith, our director of programs for Angel On A Leash, and he shadowed her on her regular visits with her dog, Fauna, at Morgan Stanley Children's Hospital. He wrote a wonderful chapter about the experience, demonstrating that he really did get it. That didn't surprise me, as I had been listening to his stories about his dogs, Scoshi and Betty, for a few years, and I knew how he loved and lived with them.

We tape the show the week before Thanksgiving at the Kennel Club of Philadelphia dog show, and then the crew comes back and edits it into a two-hour show for TV. We do the voice-over work in the studio on the Tuesday before the show airs on Thanksgiving.

NBC has been a great broadcast partner and a wonderful supporter of the concept that show dogs are real dogs. The network has always welcomed my therapy dog stories and have been supportive of Angel On A Leash as well. In fact, Rufus, the Colored Bull Terrier who was Best in Show at the National Dog Show in 2005 and at Westminster in 2006, has had his legend grow with his work as a goodwill ambassador and Angel On A Leash therapy dog for the National Dog Show since his retirement from the ring after those wins.

Cheri and I also spent a lot of time with Andrea Joyce, the great NBC sports reporter who did our backstage stories from the National Dog Show for years. Andrea was about to get a Goldendoodle, and Cheri was convincing her to make him a therapy dog. Soon Andrea was visiting at Ronald McDonald House New York with everyone's buddy, the indomitable, happy, beloved Reggie.

In 2008, the Year of Uno, United Features Syndicate invited Uno to ride on its *Peanuts* float in the Macy's Thanksgiving Day Parade, a first for a Westminster winner. I went along to be sure that he didn't fall off, one of those "other-end-of-the-leash" jobs. This experience ranked right up there for me with being on *Sex and the City*. Since our National Dog Show followed the parade, NBC gave us a great plug.

From the live telecast describing the *Peanuts* float:

Meredith Vieira: "United Features Syndicate brings us the forever-young Peanuts characters and Snoopy's doghouse. Woodstock finds high ground atop Snoopy's abode, waving flags, ready to guide the Flying Ace toward a safe landing."

Matt Lauer: "With their love of Beagles, Lucy, Linus, and Charlie Brown play with Uno—he was on our show, remember, [the] first-ever Beagle to win the Westminster dog show. Along for the ride is every dog's best friend, David Frei, host of the National Dog Show, which airs immediately following today's parade right here on NBC."

On television, you could see me waving and saying thank you to Meredith and Matt up in the booth.

And thank you to NBC.

And thank you to *Best in Show*.

We cannot put into words what it meant to Cheri and me for Belle to allow us to be the ones on the other end of her leash.

CHAPTER **13**

Calling All Angels

This passage near the end of Suzanne Clothier's wonderful book, published in 2002, says it all. Anyone who shares his or her life with a dog will have to face this reality sooner or later. It reminds us that what we get from our dogs in the relatively short time that they are with us should overcome the grief that we experience when they leave us.

> There is a cycle of love and death that shapes the lives of those who choose to travel in the company of animals. It is a cycle unlike any other. To those who have never lived through its turnings or walked its rocky path, our willingness to give our hearts with full knowledge that they will be broken seems incomprehensible. Only we know how small a price we pay for what we receive; our grief, no matter how powerful it may be, is an insufficient measure of the joy we have been given.
>
> —*Bones Would Rain from the Sky*
> Suzanne Clothier

In the spring of 2009, Belle and Teigh were both twelve years old. They were slowing down a bit, but we felt that it was just because they were twelve, not because they were having any problems. They still liked to romp and play and run at Cheri's parents' farm. Angel was starting to do some therapy dog visiting for them, but they were still spending their share of time at Sloan-Kettering and Ronald McDonald House.

One Monday night at the end of April, I noticed that Belle seemed a little distended in her abdomen. She had just eaten dinner, but it seemed to be more than that. Bloat was the first thought, so we watched her closely that night and kept her relatively quiet, but she didn't show any pain or signs of distress. However, the next night she was still distended, so I took her to Animal Medical Center (AMC). They did a number of tests and wanted more, so Cheri took her in the next day. They found fluid in her abdomen (ascites) and elevated liver enzymes and bile acid. They did a sonogram and came back with bad news: cirrhosis and atrophy of the liver. Cheri called me to share the news. We were both incredulous.

Just five months earlier, Belle had undergone a complete workup. Her blood and urine were normal, and she had been doing all of her normal activities. Now, suddenly, she was suffering, occasionally in visible pain. She was going to have to take a number of drugs, including ursodiol (a secondary bile acid), dexamethasone (a corticosteroid), omeprazole (to treat excess stomach acid), SAM-e (s-adenosyl methionine, for pain relief), and vitamin E.

Almost immediately, Belle's condition got worse. She was having trouble keeping her food down, and we adjusted the medications to try to help. She had always had a heart murmur, and we went for an EKG and chest x-rays, checking for "right side heart failure." We even consulted with a friend, who is one of the top human cardiologists in the country, in hopes of finding some help. If we could have found something going on with her heart, we would have had something to treat, something to keep her going if the liver situation was related to that.

Belle didn't look good, and she had moments when it seemed like she was looking for somewhere to curl up and die. The grim outlook from the veterinarians at AMC was that she had a couple of months to live. We were devastated by the news and devastated that she could be suffering. We wanted to do all that we could to help ease that suffering.

I immediately called Dr. Jean Dodds, a California veterinarian who is the world's leading authority on hematology, immunology, endocrinology, nutrition, and holistic medicine. I had known of Dr. Dodds for many years and was one of her disciples when it came to vaccine protocols, but I had never spoken to her directly. I was able to reach her, and she was more than willing to listen to our challenges and offer some suggestions.

We put Belle on a regimen of milk thistle and Dr. Dodds's liver-cleansing diet (white fish, potatoes, sweet potatoes, green beans, and eggs). In addition, Belle was getting about eight medications and vitamins per day.

A week later, in the middle of all of this, we all celebrated Teigh's thirteenth birthday.

The next day, unbelievably, Teigh collapsed on the sidewalk during his afternoon walk with our dog walker.

It looked to be either a stroke or a seizure, but he was having trouble breathing. He was near home, which, thank God, is only ten blocks from the AMC and only a block away from Ronald McDonald House. Cheri got to the scene quickly with friends, and they all helped get Teigh to AMC very quickly. Once there, he was intubated and sedated while the veterinarians tried to figure out what had happened. They discovered that it was a laryngeal collapse, in which the larynx is paralyzed in the closed position, making it nearly impossible to breathe. It was a bit of a miracle that he had made it the ten blocks without dying.

I joined Cheri at AMC, and soon there was much discussion with the doctors about laryngeal tieback surgery, the normal textbook treatment. But the doctors pointed out that Teigh was not a good candidate for surgery due to his age, the fact that he had pneumonia (which was an additional discovery), and the fact that he had a history of seizures. Being intubated kept him breathing and kept him alive for the moment, but decisions were going to be needed.

The doctors told us that Teigh might not even make it out of surgery if we chose that option (our only other option was euthanasia). It was our second grim outlook of the week. After a long afternoon of tests, counsel from the vets, discussion, and lots of tears and prayers, we decided to do the surgery.

We waited at AMC until the surgery was over, and they reported back at 11:30 p.m. that everything had gone according to plan, with no complications. Teigh was slow to wake up and have the breathing tube removed because he had been sedated for several hours before the surgery. The doctors were very guarded about his prognosis at this point, but we got a good report from the overnight attending veterinarian at 4 a.m.

The next afternoon, we went to visit Teigh. He was still a little groggy (so were we), but he recognized us and acknowledged us and then went peacefully to sleep again. We stayed with him for about an hour. During that time, we spoke to the doctors who had done the surgery. They said two things: that the surgery had been a success and that Teigh's recovery so far had been "miraculous"—so much so that they considered letting him come home at that point. They decided, however, that with the aspirate pneumonia that had resulted from his initial collapse on the street, and other factors, they would keep him for one more day.

Teigh was not out of danger by any means. There were lots of things going on here, keeping in mind the reasons that he was not a good candidate for the surgery in the first place. In his favor was that he was in relatively good shape for a thirteen-year-old, his weight was good, and he had a minimum of other issues. He was going blind, but that was not a factor.

This surgery consisted of taking the arytenoid cartilage (the flap that covers the windpipe) and suturing it in a permanently open position. (The PetEducation.com website has a good description of the surgery and all considerations.) Fixing the airway into a permanently open position made it possible for him to breathe, but it complicated things by creating a constant risk that food or water would get into the lungs and cause pneumonia. We would have to slow down his eating, feed him only soft foods, prohibit strenuous activities and excitement, avoid hot weather, keep him from swimming at the farm (he would drown), and have him wear a chest harness, among other precautions.

It was a long, hard week with lots of tears, lots of prayers, and not much sleep. At one point, it looked like we were going to lose both dogs rather quickly.

The next day, Teigh came home and looked pretty darn good for all that he had been through. He had a funny haircut from his surgery and a long, sutured-up incision down the front of his throat, but he was happy to be home. The doctors were very happy about everything, but they made no promises; Teigh still had a long road ahead. The first adventure came later when we gave him his first meal of meatballs—slowly!

In spite of having to learn how to eat again and all of the other restrictions, Teigh was happy and enjoying life. He sounded as of he had been debarked, but that was no surprise and was a bit entertaining when we first heard him (he didn't bark that much anyway). We felt like he was going to be around for a while.

At about this time, we got a not-so-encouraging report for Belle. Nothing showed up in the EKG, which resigned us to the fact that it was liver failure, and we were dealing with palliative care only at this point.

Amid all of these challenges, it was interesting to watch Angel, our Cavalier. She seemed to sense that something was going on with each of other dogs and was being very respectful about space, lying quietly next to them on their beds instead of being her normal sassy little self.

For the next few weeks, Teigh's recovery and Belle's battle continued. By the end of May, one month after her original diagnosis, we were convinced that Belle was getting a little better every day, one day at a time. Her appetite was voracious, we were feeding her four or five times a day, and she was always looking for food. Her ascites seemed to have gone away, and she did not seem to have the discomfort that she had been fighting from the beginning.

She was happy and trotting down the hall, even breaking into a gallop occasionally. She would go to her toy box and find something to play with. She could be a little wobbly on her feet and was losing some muscle mass; this was especially evident in the rear legs. She couldn't jump up onto the couch like she once did, but we got some of those doggy stairs for her, and she learned to use them.

She would occasionally have some upswings, once perking up a bit after a visit to AMC in the afternoon. We walked (very slowly) the ten blocks home, and she was out at the end of the lead.

"We're gonna keep battling," I wrote to her veterinarian. "She had a good morning, and I want to believe that she is going to have a little better morning tomorrow ... one day at a time is fine with us."

As it turned out, one day at a time was all that we got.

On Tuesday, a couple of days after our AMC visit, Belle suddenly stopped eating. She couldn't keep any of her medications down. We tried everything, but when I carried her out to relieve herself that Saturday night, it was evident that the end was coming.

Belle passed on peacefully early Sunday morning, June 7, 2009. I had slept on the floor next to her that night, and I had followed her around on the floor as she had moved a couple of times during the night; the last time was at around 5:30 a.m., when she moved to a position behind the chair where Cheri was sleeping. I think Belle probably wanted to say goodbye to her. I woke up at 6:30 a.m. to find that she had left us. We took her to Cheri's parents' farm in New Jersey that afternoon and buried her there on a beautiful country day. It was devastating, as we had believed that she had been getting a little bit better every day for the past month.

What a wonderful life Belle had lived! Cheri had brought Belle and Teigh to me, and Belle was my first therapy dog—there would certainly be no Angel On A Leash if not for her. She did so much for so many and taught me so much in her nine years of visiting Ronald McDonald House, Memorial Sloan-Kettering, homeless people on the streets, all here in New York City; Bailey-Bouchay AIDS Hospice in Seattle; and many more facilities and individuals.

Along the way, Belle had a few adventures. She broke her jaw and almost died when she was hit by a train as a puppy in Washington. She lived through an earthquake with me in Seattle as things were crashing down all around us in the apartment (Teigh and Cheri were out visiting somewhere). She ran off the dock into Lake Union chasing ducks and attended Mass at New York City's famous St. Patrick's Cathedral. She got sprayed by a skunk on the move from Seattle to New York. And she captured her AKC Junior Hunter and Canine Good Citizen titles, finally getting around to finishing her conformation championship at the grand age of six.

We cannot put into words what it meant to Cheri and me for Belle to have allowed us to us be the ones on the other end of her leash. How blessed we have been.

As we drove away from the family farm that night, the song "Calling All Angels" by Train came on the radio. We drove home through the tears.

· · · · · ·

It seemed as if I had just finally finished thanking everyone for their wonderful support for Belle and for us when the next blow landed in mid-June. At the time of his emergency surgery, the doctors of course took Teigh's blood, and they found that his liver enzymes were elevated. They said then that it could have been because he was oxygen-deprived at the time, and his liver may have been reacting to that, but we all wanted to have him checked again.

So after Belle passed, I took Teigh to AMC for an ultrasound, and unbelievably, his ultrasound showed that he, too, was in the early stages of cirrhosis. He wasn't as far along as Belle had been when she was diagnosed, and he had a larger liver at the moment, so things might be different for him, we hoped.

He had a biopsy done, via ultrasound, which we could not do with Belle because she was too far along and did not have enough liver tissue to biopsy. The biopsy came back inconclusive. His bloodwork showed everything to be normal except for elevated liver enzymes. I spoke to Dr. Jean Dodds for her counsel, and we put Teigh on Dr. Dodds's liver-cleansing diet, which Belle had been on, and milk thistle.

This was a little alarming, to say the least. Teigh and Belle were out of the same dam, but different sires (but the sires were brothers). But what if it was something environmental? We immediately got Angel checked out, and ourselves, as well. We were all fine, but we will always wonder if there was some environmental factor that caused Teigh's and Belle's liver problems.

So we found ourselves asking for prayers for Teigh. It just did not seem quite fair to him, and, once again, we set out to battle this thing with all we had.

Teigh was trotting around the halls of our apartment building and seemed in good spirits. We had to keep reminding ourselves that he was thirteen and could just be slow some days because of his age, not to mention his recent major surgery. Because Teigh's liver disease was not as far along as Belle's had been when we diagnosed it, we were being as aggressive as we could be. We were guarded about our optimism, however, after being fooled about Belle's progress in the first few weeks.

In the meantime, life went on. The two veterinarians who had worked on Teigh graduated from Animal Medical Center's Intern and Resident Class about this time. Dr. Jamie Warren, who saved Teigh's life when he came into triage that day, was named "Intern of the Year" and was heading to Oregon (in an amazing coincidence, to Eugene, my hometown); and the surgery resident, Dr. Nicole Buote, who did his surgery, was going to Los Angeles to work at the California Animal Hospital. We will always remember what they did, what they said, how they performed when we really needed it. We went to their graduation and felt like proud parents.

By late summer, Teigh's laryngeal tieback surgery was only a memory, and he seemed to be fighting off the liver issues. But then, abruptly, he hit the wall, and we thought that the end was coming. Like Belle, he seemingly had been getting a little better each day. But then, also like Belle, he suddenly stopped eating. He looked like a noodle and just seemed the same as Belle had been right before she died.

We were frantic. We got him to AMC, and they were again quite grim about the outlook. We added some medications and started feeding him baby food: beef, green beans, peas, sweet potatoes, and pasta. He loved it, and all of this helped him battle his way back. Once we adjusted his medications and got him eating, he came charging back. We found Dr. Dodds's diet in cans, and he loved it; he seemed better than he had been before his diagnosis.

We were now guardedly optimistic. Teigh was trotting down the hall, playing with Angel, eating enthusiastically, and looking just like he did six months earlier, before all of this had happened. It was unbelievable.

We had to keep reminding ourselves that Teigh just might be slowing down with age, as well as from his disease, but he was happy and in no apparent pain. He was becoming blinder, too, but that didn't bother him. The aftereffect of the throat surgery was that he did not do well in the heat, so I couldn't let him walk when the weather was hot, and I had to keep him from getting too excited in general.

We would take Teigh to Finnegan's, his favorite sidewalk restaurant in the neighborhood, pulling him in a Red Flyer wagon. I never thought I would be one of those dog owners who I perceived to be a bit wacky, but Teigh was doing great, and I promised to do whatever it took. I also promised to never again make fun of the lady who puts shoes on her Yorkie.

Angel became totally attached to Teigh. We made the decision to get another Brittany, a puppy whose paternal grandfather was Belle's litter brother. A lot of tears were still being shed for Belle, as well as in anticipation of what was happening with Teigh. A puppy would be good for all of us; we needed to get busy again in the therapy dog world. Teigh was retired, and Angel was a little better with the ladies at Sloan-Kettering than with the poking and prodding and body slams from the kids at Ronald McDonald House.

So Grace came home with us in early October, at the age of eight weeks, and we imagined her receiving Brittany wisdom from Teigh in his final days.

Teigh began a downhill slide in December. We finally took him off all of his medications in hopes that he would stop vomiting and having diarrhea, and that maybe he would have some quiet days at the end. I was afraid that we were making him sick every day with his meds. He had stopped eating his cream cheese, which we used to deliver his pills, and I thought that he may have been associating that with being sick. After all, his daily list was fourteen items long, ranging from vitamins to SAM-e to colchicine to ondansetron to Pepcid and more. I knew that each thing had a purpose, but the sum total was making him miserable.

Teigh still had an appetite, he would respond to certain things, but mostly he was lethargic and slow. He was showing some ascites, he had a racing heart from time to time, his breathing was very irregular, and he had diarrhea and concentrated urine. He was wobbly on his feet, falling occasionally into walls, and he couldn't jump on the couch when it used to be effortless for him.

It was time.

We asked one of our veterinarians to come to our apartment one evening in January to help us give Teigh some permanent peace. We wanted him to go at home, surrounded by people who had been with him and had helped him through his life.

We had convinced ourselves, but really Teigh also had to convince us that this was the right thing. The peaceful but pleading look in his eyes did it. We had dealt with all of the counsel from friends and family, and it was now on us. Teigh had had a great life and had done great things for so many people—most of all, for us. We owed him so much; we owed him his dignity, freedom from pain, and a peaceful passing.

• • • • • •

On Saturday, January 9, 2010, we sent this message to our friends and family:

> May 4, 1996–January 9, 2010
> Teigh passed at home tonight, peacefully and with dignity. May he rest in peace, whatever peace he can find now that he is reunited with his sister, Belle.
>
> He leaves a wonderful legacy. As a star therapy dog, he made a difference in the lives of the thousands of people he visited over the years at:
>
> • Bailey-Boushay AIDS Hospice (Seattle)
> • Providence Medical Center (Seattle)
> • Mt. Sinai Hospital (New York)

- NewYork-Presbyterian—Cornell (New York)
- Morgan Stanley Children's Hospital (New York)
- Terence Cardinal Cooke Health Care Center (New York)
- Ronald McDonald House (New York City)
- Memorial Sloan-Kettering Cancer Center (New York City)
- ...and others

He received lots of awards and recognition. He helped open doors for therapy dogs in many places. He was the first dog allowed in the Bone Marrow Transplant unit at New York Hospital; the first dog to visit at the Ronald McDonald House in New York City, helping to create a thriving therapy dog program there; the first therapy dog allowed to visit in-room at Mt. Sinai; and he was part of a historic pilot program that brought the first dogs ever allowed at Sloan-Kettering.

He made people smile—a simple thing, really, but something that had a huge impact when it happened with kids with cancer, paraplegics in wheelchairs or beds, women fighting devastating but hopeful battles with cancer, or homeless people sleeping on cardboard on the streets of New York.

He did lots of media appearances to support his work for Angel On A Leash and Delta Society, including the *Today Show*, *Good Morning America*, *Martha Stewart*, and others. His best media performance was probably rolling over on the mall for the *Today Show* to introduce a weather report.

And most of all, of course, he was a wonderful friend and member of the family. Rest in peace, T-Boy; we love you and we'll be with you and Belle again someday.

David and Cheri

• • • • • •

We were devastated by the loss of Belle and Teigh—we still are, and we think about them every day. But when we do, we smile.

Teigh and Belle changed my life. And they touched a lot of other people, too.

" This was another of those times where nothing needed to be said; I could just let Angel carry the moment....Everyone was crying and I was fighting back tears myself. 'Godspeed, sweetie. God loves you, and so does Angel.' "

My Angels Have Four Legs

In 2007, Cheri and I decided that we were going to add a Cavalier to our Brittany household. This was not because of Elizabeth Taylor, but because Teigh and Belle were slowing down and couldn't visit as much as they had been. We didn't think we could handle a third active Brittany in our one-bedroom, high-rise apartment (note: *active* is the word you use when it is your dog; *hyper* is the word to describe another person's dog acting the same way as your *active* dog).

For several years, I had been serving as the emcee/auctioneer at the American Cavalier King Charles Spaniel Club (ACKCSC)'s fund-raising auction, held at its national specialty show. The auction raises money for the club's charitable trust, which provides financial and other support for charitable, educational, and health research efforts for Cavaliers. There are a number of breed parent clubs that have foundations for health studies, which try to find causes and treatments for health issues that might exist in their respective breeds. It's research *for* the dogs, not *on* the dogs, and the parent clubs have made progress of which they should be proud. The ACKCSC is among those clubs that are doing it right, and I was glad to be able to help them raise a lot of money each year.

Over the years, we had made a lot of Cavalier friends. We had come to love the breed and had done our homework, just as I always preach to everyone on my television shows, and now we were finally ready to get one of these cute little dogs for ourselves.

One evening, we had both Teigh and Belle with us at Ronald McDonald House, and we mentioned that we were going to add another dog to our family, a smaller one so that everyone could hold her on their laps.

"What is her name?" one of the kids asked.

"We don't know yet; we haven't decided."

"How about Sophia?" came the first suggestion, opening the floodgates.

"Angel!"

"Truffle!"

"Fleur!"

"Bon Bon!"

"Those are all good suggestions," Cheri told them. "Why don't we have a contest?" And so we did. Cheri put a ballot box in the playroom with a photo of the yet unnamed Cavalier puppy on it. With an international population at the House, we got a lot of fun entries, but in the end, "Angel" was the winner.

Angel joined the family later that year, coming as a gift from our dear friend Patty Kanan, a great Cavalier breeder from California. Angel was five months old, and her registered name became Torlundy Courtlore Angel Eyes. Patty kept the theme going by naming the male in the litter Torlundy Courtlore Johnny Angel.

Angel was a Blenheim, the same orange-and-white color pattern as the Brittanys, giving them together the appearance of family. We got the occasional "Is that their puppy?" inquiry from people on the streets as we walked all three of them.

Angel fit right in with the family. She was a feisty little princess, probably equal parts feisty and princess. She didn't need to be too feisty because Teigh and Belle welcomed her readily (well, Belle would look at her sideways once in a while). Angel loved everyone she met. We got her into therapy dog class right away even though she couldn't be registered until she was a year old. She flew right through the class at the ASPCA, and Michele Siegel, the instructor, loved her (OK, I admit it, she was probably the teacher's pet). Angel passed everything and became a registered therapy dog as soon as she turned one. She was a big hit wherever she went and a great part of the family.

I love Angel dearly. She's the first little dog I've ever had, and it's been fun. It's nice to have a dog who fits into a shoulder bag and can get on a subway or bus or into a cab with no questions. The shoulder bag brings a lot of photo opportunities, too: Angel peeking out of the top, sleeping in the bag with the front panel open, and more. I also am able to bring her along, unannounced, in her bag, to a number of other places (wink, wink).

Bringing it back to *Sex and the City*, we visit Sloan-Kettering's tenth floor—the women's health unit—every Monday night, carrying on for Teigh and Belle. There, our audience is female and nearly the same demographic as the audience for the TV show. We get a number of patients who remember the specific episode of the show.

"Is that Elizabeth Taylor?" Sometimes they start to figure it out on their own: "Hey, you were in that show, too, weren't you?"

Angel's first stop on her Monday night visits is always at the nurses' station, where she might show the nurses a few tricks and get them smiling and laughing, which is a nice break for them from a tough job. A few of the nurses up there refer to her as "Elizabeth Taylor," too.

Angel will happily launch into her trick routine for the nurses. "What's your best trick?" I'll ask, and boom, she rolls over. It's not just a lazy rollover, it's at full speed, as she knows that a treat awaits her. She will often do this without any prompting because she senses that when the crowd gathers, it's for her performance. She even did it in the show ring once. Angel was in the lineup of open bitches, looking up at Cheri, who made a move as if she had some kind of treat in her hand. Boom! Rollover. People at ringside laughed, so she did it again.

Back to Sloan-Kettering. "What else can you do?" She jumps in the air and does a twisting flip. That is the most athletic move in her routine, and she does that without much prompting, either. When she stops and sits, I'll hold out my hand and say, "Give me five!" and she puts her paw into my hand. Worth a few treats.

It's certainly entertaining, and I even let her special buddy, Cathy, one of the nurses, put her through the routine. My only reluctance is that I don't want to get Angel too excited right before she goes in to visit a patient. I don't want her to be looking to me for treats all the time, so I rarely use them in the room with a patient. When we're done with the nurses, I take a few seconds to show Angel that I don't have any more treats and let her know that now it's time to get to work.

One afternoon, we were part of a photo shoot on the tenth floor for the therapy dog calendar that the hospital publishes each year. Angel came out in a scrub suit, and business came to a halt. She had on a hat, mask, and gown, and she and her French Bulldog buddy, Cooper, drew a three-deep crowd of spectators—medical people, patients, and visitors—as she and the Frenchie posed for their calendar pictures.

Angel is quite photogenic and also has been on a few television shows and news stories. She was featured with me in a February 2011 *New York Magazine* piece, and we found out just how many of our friends read the magazine because we got a lot of notes and emails commenting on the adorable picture of Angel in my arms.

Most important to what Angel does, being the size that she is, is that she fits right into the beds at Memorial Sloan-Kettering with patients who need her, with women who have been through or are facing major, life-changing surgeries. Often, when we walk into a room, the patient starts to make room in her bed for Angel.

We never know what we are going to find when we walk into a room at Sloan-Kettering. The census that we get at the start of the visit only says "yes" or "no" next to each patient's name, indicating how the patients responded to the canvasser earlier in the day about a visit from a therapy dog later. The patient might be there for a checkup, for treatment, for surgery, or for something else. She may have had her surgery already or may be getting ready for surgery the next day.

Some of the patients are in good spirits, some are hurting, and some are scared. They may have been here before, they may have just gotten here, or they may have been here for a week. It's not my job to ask them about any of that. We are there to visit in the moment, to give them something to think about and talk about other than the challenges that they may be facing, to give them something to smile about.

It's obvious when the outlook is grim or, worse, when someone is getting ready to die. Often, the room is filled with people, and the patient is weak. Often, the patient still wants to see Angel, or her family members may want to get Angel in there to give them all one final smiling moment.

One night, we walked into a room, and there must have been twelve people in there, breaking rules that were meant to be broken at a time like this. Parents, husband, children, sisters, brothers, friends. They all reacted to Angel. I recognized the patient as someone we had seen the previous week, and I knew her name from the census anyway, so I greeted her by name.

"Hi, Reina. You really have a full house tonight. Is this a good time for a visit from us?" That question was really directed at the family, who probably knew best what was right for the moment.

"Yes," she said softly. "Yes," said several of the others in the room, and they made a path for us to get to Reina's side. I could hear lots of sniffles and soft crying. My guess was that they had all been called to Reina's bedside.

"Is this Angel?" one of them asked.

"Yes. Did Reina tell you about Angel?" I asked.

"She told us all about her. She loves Angel, and we are so glad you are here," came an answer.

"Well, we are glad, too. Let's see if we can fit her in here."

I laid down our towel on the bed. I could see a few tubes, and I knew that Reina was so fragile that it didn't make any difference if she had any sutures—I was going to have to be very careful to keep Angel off of her.

I set Angel down at Reina's side. I could hear and see cell-phone cameras shooting away, and I could hear a little more crying, almost happy crying, as they saw Reina reacting to Angel.

Reina smiled, and I took her hand, placing it on Angel's neck. "How's that?" I asked. She smiled to indicate that it was just fine. She tried to sit up a little more, but it hurt her. "Just stay right there; we will get her to you," I said. Her husband helped her move a little bit. I got Angel to lie down along Reina's side, and she sat quietly, looking right at Reina.

This was another of those times where nothing needed to be said; I could just let Angel carry the moment. I was giving all of my attention and energy to keeping Angel right where she was and keeping Reina's hand on her. Reina was smiling and speaking softly to Angel in Spanish. I was thinking that, tonight, Angel was understanding everything Reina was saying, even in Spanish. Her tail was wagging softly, and that got an audible reaction and a few more tears from the room.

Reina didn't have much strength at this point, and after several minutes I kind of felt that Angel and I should move along and give the family their time with her. I knew she wasn't going to last much longer.

I said a little prayer for Reina to myself, squeezed her hand gently, and then gathered Angel up. Reina smiled and said thank you and then tried to lean forward to Angel. I moved Angel closer. Reina softly put her hand on Angel's head, and I lifted Angel up to eye level. Reina drew Angel to her and kissed her. Angel licked her face.

Everyone was crying, and I was fighting back tears myself. "Godspeed, sweetie. God loves you, and so does Angel."

• • • • • •

It's the nature of the job, of course, and the places we visit that we find ourselves dealing with death too often. We usually are not there, intentionally or unintentionally, to witness someone's actual passing. For one thing, Sloan-Kettering moves the patients through the tenth floor quickly. Most of the people we visit there on our regular Monday night visits are gone—we hope home— by the time of our next visit on the following Monday. We can see death coming, though, and occasionally our patients tell us that they are being moved to hospice the next day because nothing more can be done for them at the hospital, but that's as close as we come.

It's a different story at Ronald McDonald House, mostly because many of the families are there for weeks or months or even years. As the director of family support, Cheri goes to work there every day and grows close to the children and their families over time. While I don't go every day, I usually get there more than once a week for visits and events, and I see the same kids often. The "I only come once a week; I hope to never see you here again" line from MSK doesn't work here. You can't help but build relationships, and too often those relationships end up being painful.

Cheri is often the one to preside over a death and/or a memorial service and all that goes with it. We find ourselves battling right alongside the children and their families, praying, hoping, and praying some more. But it's a different story here because these are kids. It's difficult to understand how this miserable disease in its many forms targets children. No, it is not fair.

Cheri and I don't have children of our own. Yes, our dogs are our children, and we fight every battle that they fight when it comes to their health. We don't usually share those struggles with the families at the House because of what they are going through themselves, but that doesn't change anything for us and our dogs.

Belle passed just after Angel turned two years old. We were devastated. Angel helped us get through it. We knew that she would be carrying on for Belle—not replacing Belle, but carrying on. That helped a little.

It was hard to tell the kids at the House, and we didn't tell many of them. They had their own battles, and we didn't want to burden them with one more. We told some of the parents, giving them the option of how, if at all, they would tell the kids. We still could bring Angel and Teigh to visit; it just wouldn't be Belle's turn on this night.

When you are visible in the neighborhood, as all of us with dogs can be, certain things happen when you go through the loss of one of your family members. We all know that it could happen to us next, and we want to say and do the right thing to be supportive. We say it and do it while looking at our own dogs, thinking about the day that it will be them and about how much our own dogs mean to us. So we actually get a double dose of sadness: one for our friend and his or her dog, and one for ourselves and our own dogs.

The news about Belle spread quickly around the neighborhood. It happened with Belle just like it happens with all of them. Our friends, accustomed to seeing us with three dogs, would now see us out with two, and couldn't help but ask, "Where's Belle?" Sometimes they didn't ask, but instead would look at us like they knew, they had heard, or they had seen us carrying her out of our building wrapped in a blanket. The first go-round can often be a wordless hug.

I found myself telling Belle's story a lot, and I was happy to do it, difficult as it may have been. Well, why not? She was a great dog, a great member of our family, and beloved in the neighborhood. She went too early, but she had a full life, and I didn't mind sharing that with people. God rest her orange-and-white soul.

After Belle's passing, we talked about getting another Brittany. With Angel, we had the perfect therapy dog for the hospital: a Cavalier that was cute—beyond cute—and of a smaller size that enabled her to do some things that a 35-pound Brittany might not be able to do as easily, such as fit into bed with a patient. Another plus was the ability to get Angel to the hospital when the weather was bad; she never had to put a foot on the ground between our apartment and the hospital if need be. We could get her there and not have to clean her feet or wipe her down when we got there. We couldn't haul Teigh that far.

Anyway, by now Teigh wasn't well and really wasn't doing any serious visiting. Most of his adventures came when we loaded him into his red wagon and took him to

Finnegan's Wake for dinner and social time.

We decided that we would look for a young Brittany, not a puppy, hopeful that we could avoid playing the high-rise house-training games and get her into therapy dog class right away. We put the word out that we were looking for a young female that would be a show prospect, but our first priority was therapy dog mentality. We looked at a few when I judged at the Brittany national specialty in Colorado that summer, but we didn't find the right match.

Then we got an email from some friends who had just bred a litter. They admitted that they knew we were looking for an older dog, but they pointed out that this litter's grandsire was Belle's litter brother Jake, and they thought that we might be interested.

So much for plans. When we heard that, it was the end of our search. What better tribute to Belle than to carry on with her legacy?

We went to New Hampshire to see the litter at four weeks of age. We were immediately drawn to the largest puppy, who was quite dominant. We tentatively picked her, then went back three weeks later to confirm, then brought her home when she was eight weeks old.

We named her Grace (officially, Triumphant's Healing Grace), and she fit in right away—literally, as she could run underneath Angel. She grew up very nicely over the next few months, very respectful of Teigh and his condition but romping with Angel. It was very touching to see her lying on the couch next to Teigh and Angel, who was also quite protective of Teigh and sensitive to him.

Grace, however, soon had her own battle to fight. Because of a mix-up with her vaccines, she had been left unprotected and got parvovirus just as we were in the thick of battling every day for Teigh. Grace was in isolation and intensive care at AMC on Christmas Eve and Christmas Day, and, of course, we were right there with her as much as we were allowed. We couldn't believe it, but we had caught it in time and got her through it. When she came home, she had to spend two weeks in isolation in our apartment, never going outside during that time.

Grace was growing up to be very sweet, not quite as crazed as Teigh and Belle were as puppies. We blame that on her bout with parvo and also on the fact that she was being raised in a high-rise apartment in Manhattan with a Toy dog. She was still showing her bird dog heritage, pointing every pigeon she came across, and she ran with abandon up and down our hallway, but she wasn't quite as intense about life as Teigh and Belle had been. Actually, I think that was a good thing.

It wasn't long after Grace's bout with parvo that Teigh was facing his final days. Angel and Grace were both especially protective of him on his last day; they seemed to know what was coming. When he finally did pass at home on a Saturday night, they mourned quietly and stayed right by his side.

Angel and Grace both came out to the farm on that Sunday morning to watch us bury Teigh next to Belle. The two of them were in the spirit of the occasion, and they spent some time lying on the graves.

We didn't feel like we were starting over, but life was going to be so much different without Teigh and Belle. We weren't asking Angel and Grace to replace them, but we did talk to them about carrying on for Teigh and Belle. They have not disappointed us or anyone else.

The Angel by My Side

The Angel By My Side: The True Story of a Dog Who Saved a Man...and a Man Who Saved a Dog is a book that I wrote with Mike Lingenfelter. It is the compelling, award-winning story of a 98-pound, red-haired, four-legged angel named Dakota ("Cody"), a story that encompasses health, science, spirituality, and the metaphysical.

Dakota changed people's lives, especially Mike's life. In 1995, Mike was ready for his life to be over and was even considering ending it himself. Two serious heart attacks and open-heart surgeries had taken away most of the good things in his life. His doctors still held out hope for him, and they were trying to find ways to motivate Mike to get out and exercise. Their vision was that an energetic dog on a leash might just do that.

And so it was that a Golden Retriever named Dakota, who himself had been rescued from death, came to help Mike with his rehabilitative therapy. Dakota had overcome many obstacles in life, from his beginnings as a sickly abandoned dog to his own battle with cancer.

But, along the way, he became a heroic service dog.

Dakota became Mike's protector and best friend, saving Mike's life several times by alerting on Mike to warn him of oncoming heart attacks and unstable angina episodes, sensing them even before Mike himself could. Dakota's unique ability enabled Mike to take his medication early enough to head off the worst effects of the attacks.

With that, Dakota gave Mike back his dignity, his pride, and his life. With his attacks now under control, Mike was able to go back to his career as a highly decorated and sought-after engineer, designing radio communication systems for airports, mass transit systems, and other public carriers worldwide. Dakota came with him, watching over Mike vigilantly, and also, amazingly, saving the lives of a couple of Mike's colleagues.

Seeing Dakota's special gift, Mike readily and happily shared him with others through animal-assisted activities, seeing it as his duty to show the world the power of the human-animal bond. Their work included visits to pediatric patients in hospitals, to special needs children in schools, to a camp for kids with cancer, and to seniors in extended care. Dakota and Mike were widely recognized as a very special team, teaching lessons about hope and happiness and inner peace. They won many awards for their tireless efforts.

Ironically, after making all of these miracles happen for Mike and after giving so much to others through the years, ultimately Dakota needed a miracle for himself.

From the book:

After a while, the door to the exam room finally opened, and Dr. Krug waved us in. Dakota was sitting there, peacefully.

Dr. Krug had tears in his eyes. "I didn't want to be right. I wanted to find something else, but it's cancer."

Thoughts fired rapidly through my brain: *Cancer?! Cancer now, after all he's been through? After all we've been through? How can this be? Where are you, God? How can you let this happen to him? All Dakota has ever done is help people. How can you do this to me, God? To us? To my family?*

I was suddenly angry. I wanted to hit something. If Dakota has cancer, *I* have cancer.

"It's a death sentence, Mike," Dr. Krug said, somewhere through my anger. "I'm not going to lie to you. You're looking at four to six weeks, maybe three months, tops. I didn't want to find a tumor, but here it is." He put the x-ray up on the light screen. The tumor was the large white circle in the middle of the picture. It looked like a headlight coming straight at me, full speed ahead.

Within a week, we had gotten Dakota to the best place he could be. From the book:

There was little doubt that Dr. Greg Ogilvie was "The Man" and the Animal Cancer Center (ACC) at Colorado State University (CSU) in Fort Collins was "The Mountain."

If your dog or cat has cancer, this is the place to be. The ACC is widely acknowledged as the world's leading research and treatment facility for cancer in animals, and Dr. Ogilvie is the world's leading authority. The work being done on animals at CSU also had profound implications in the field of human cancer.

Nancy [Mike's wife] and I found out that Dr. Ogilvie was a great believer in the human-animal bond, which pretty much sold us on him before we even showed up there. We'd heard over and over again about his passion for his work and his compassion for his patients and their people.

Everyone we spoke to about him said he was a legend, larger than life.

He was even better in person.

We had a bit of an entourage as we walked through the door of the clinic that morning with Dakota—there was the three-person crew from *Good Morning America* lugging a TV camera and a boom mike on their shoulders, Dana Durrance from the Argus Institute's Support Program, Dr. Harold Krug, and me.

Dr. Ogilvie approached the group and introduced himself by saying, "Somebody here has to be Dakota's dad."

"That's me, sir," I said. We humans all exchanged a few pleasantries, and then Dr. Ogilvie got down on his hands and knees on the waiting room floor and greeted Dakota as if he were a long-lost friend.

"Hey, Dakota, how are you doing?" His hands were stroking Dakota's head, neck, back, and chest. I bet that Cody was already feeling better. He did a quick initial exam on the floor, checking his vital signs and the like, and then led us back into an exam room.

I already knew that I was seeing the best in action.

"How are *you* holding up, Mike?" he asked me.

"It's pretty rough, Dr. Ogilvie," I told him. "I can't lie to you—this big guy means the world to me, in many different ways."

"First of all, call me Greg. You are now part of the family here."

Yes, he is the very best, I thought.

"Cancer is an emotional disease, Mike. It steals hope, and once you lose hope, your life is violated and you feel totally out of control."

He was right about that.

"By the time people get to us with their pets, they're scared to death. They're afraid that there are no options left for them and their pets, that it's time for the holy water "

I could understand that. "Things do seem a little grim—three months to live kind of got our attention."

"Well, let's not kid about this," he said. "Cancer is the number-one natural cause of death in dogs and cats in the US. As for the type of cancer that Dakota has, the average dog will live only a few months unless they get some prompt care."

I was sitting down with Dakota's head in my lap, trying unsuccessfully to hold back the tears. I've never been good at that when it comes to Dakota.

Dr. Ogilvie saw my emotion and tried to reassure me. "Remember, I see more lymphoma in a couple of weeks' time than most practitioners do in a lifetime. That gives us a real advantage. Believe it or not, cancer is the most curable of all common diseases."

I'd never heard anyone say that about cancer, and here I was hearing it from the world's leading authority. I was riveted to Dr. Ogilvie's words.

"There isn't a single patient that we can't help," Dr. Ogilvie continued, "and we're going to help Dakota. We're going to get him back to you with a minimum of downtime, ready to be back in your life soon. We've come a long way. Back in the day that I was educated, there were very few options for cancer patients. The mentality was that cancer is a disease, that you either cure it or you die of it. The reality today is that it doesn't have to be that way anymore. If we can't cure it, many cancers can be controlled for a long period of time.

"And why is that so hard to grasp? We're now defining *cancer* as a chronic disease. You think nothing of having a heart valve replaced if you have heart disease, or getting a kidney transplant or dialysis if you have renal disease—the comparisons can go on and on. We can put cancer in remission. It may take time, and it may require a number of different treatment modalities that can be difficult, but the truth is that we can do something here, much more than just make the patient comfortable in preparation for death. We don't accept that. That's not what we do. So there you have it, Mike. That's my pep talk, and now it's time to get to work."

My heart was pounding away—but it must have been pounding in a good way, because Dakota wasn't alerting on me. I wanted to jump up out of my chair and shout, "I believe!"

As the battle raged, Mike discovered, through the help of an animal communicator and his own observations, that Dakota was a spirit guide, a guardian angel seemingly here on Earth to watch over Mike. From the book, the following is the first encounter between Dakota and Dr. Brenda McClelland (animal communicator) in Colorado. Mike and Nancy were there to observe.

[Brenda] got down on her knees next to Cody as he sprawled on the floor, closed her eyes, and held her hands over him. Immediately, he started inhaling in such a way that his chest was raising a good 6 inches with each breath, which, by itself, was already pretty amazing. I stole a look at Nancy and saw that her eyes were open wide in disbelief, but we both sat quietly. It seemed like an eternity, but it was in reality only about four or five minutes until Brenda opened her eyes and dropped her arms. Cody's breathing quickly returned to normal.

"Wow," she said. We waited for more.

"I feel bizarre telling you this," Brenda said. "I don't know your background, I don't know what you believe, but this is not a dog. This is a spirit guide in a dog's body."

"What's a spirit guide?" I asked.

"Well, some people might think of them as angels—they follow us around and sort of hang around up there in the subconscious and help us. My Catholic upbringing won't let me call them angels, because I think of angels as unattainable." She paused. "I knew it the moment I connected with Dakota—there was so much energy there, it was different from an ordinary animal. It really hit me, and I knew right away that he was a spirit guide."

Nancy and I weren't much help here. We didn't know what to say.

"I've come across spirit guides many times before," Brenda continued, "hanging around in the subconscious, but this is the first one that I've found actually residing in an animal or a human. I suspect that there could be others around, but this is the first time I've seen it in thirteen years of doing this. Spirit guides are all around us, floating about—some people might call them guardian angels. They sometimes save your life and then disappear, but Dakota chose to take a physical form that was going to be here for a lifetime before moving on.

At that point, Nancy jumped in. "What's he doing here?"

"He's here to protect Mike and watch over him. Dakota is his guardian angel."

No one spoke for a moment while that sank in. Finally, Nancy broke the silence. "Where did he come from?"

"I asked him, and he said, 'I am not from this material world.' He sounds a little cocky to me, but I've heard that attitude before. Here on Earth, we're kind of lagging behind in the spiritual world."

"Why is he here as a dog?" I had to ask.

"He said he specifically came as a dog hoping

to get people to see animals in different light, as spiritual beings. He wants to raise the status of animals in society, to show that they have consciousness, too, that they're more than dumb creatures. So in a sense, the dog has a larger purpose in mind, and he's using you to get his message across. He says that this is going to be hard for a lot of people, because in most religions, people have dominion over animals." Brenda took a deep breath. "I'm going back for more."

We witnessed the same scene once again, only this time it lasted a little longer. I'd never seen anything like this. Cody was taking in so much air that I thought he was going to raise up off the carpet. This time Brenda delivered our message to Dakota. He responded by telling her things that only he and I knew about, things I'd never even shared with Nancy.

"Dakota says that you need to stop worrying, that he knows that you love him. He wants you to stop worrying about him, and he doesn't want you to think about the same kind of stuff that you were thinking about that first night back in Dallas at the hotel."

I knew exactly what Brenda was talking about. Dakota and I had gone to Dallas to start work, and Nancy was going to join us later. The night before my first day back on the job, I was having some misgivings about going back to work, the move, and life in general, and in the hotel room, I spoke to Dakota about it. He never answered me ... until now.

> Brenda said that she found Dakota to be extremely down-to-earth, and based on his vibration, she felt that he he'd been around for a long time in other forms. She called him a wise, old soul.

In spite of Dr. Ogilvie's best efforts and Dakota's courageous battle, the end came too soon—a year and a half later—in October of 2001. With Mike always at the other end of the leash, Dakota had shown others how to live with dignity and, at the end, how to die with dignity.

Dakota's legacy is huge. Whether he was making children smile or take a step or talk, or helping senior citizens find a final peace, Dakota was truly a very special dog. More than a dog, actually, he was an angel with a very special power to help those he touched.

Dakota and Mike were named 1999 Service Dog Team of the Year by Delta Society. Dakota was elected to the Texas Veterinary Medical Foundation Animal Hall of Fame, chosen as Humanitarian of the Year by the Sertoma Club of Dallas (the first non-human recipient in history), and inducted into the Alabama Veterinary Medicine Association Animal Hall of Fame.

Dakota's story has been featured on *Good Morning America*, the USA Network, the Discovery Channel, and the PAX Network; in the *Seattle Times*, the *Dallas Morning News*, the *Denver Post*, the *Huntsville Times*, and the Knight Ridder newspaper syndicate; and in the book *The Healing Power of Pets* by Dr. Marty Becker.

The Angel By My Side, published in 2002, won two awards from the Dog Writers Association of America. The book is still available in trade paperback through various sources.

Yorkie Doodle Dandy

The most wonderful things happen to me because of my life in dogs. Here's a story that has come to me in pieces over the years and has impacted me in a lot of ways.

In the mid-1990s, I was asked to guest host the show *Pet News* on the Fox News Channel, sitting in for my friend Brian Kilcommons, the great dog trainer. It was a two-hour show that included interviews and features from the world of pets. My invitation came from Chet Collier, who in addition to being president of Westminster, was an executive vice president of Fox News.

The show was shot at the Fox News studios in New York and was live on Saturday morning, repeated on tape on Sunday morning. It was indeed a "variety" show, featuring dogs, cats, fish, reptiles, birds, shelters, charities, you name it. I even hosted a doggy wedding one of the times that I was there.

One of my guests one week was a gentleman named Bill Wynne. Bill had served in the US Army Air Corps in World War II and was based in the South Pacific as an aerial photographer. One of his GI buddies had found a Yorkshire Terrier, of all things, in a foxhole in New Guinea, and Bill bought her for about $6.

Bill named the dog Smoky, and they became inseparable companions, with Smoky traveling in Bill's duffel bag and accompanying him on twelve combat missions. Bill was on the show to tell the story of Smoky, as chronicled in his book, *Yorkie Doodle Dandy*.

While we think of military dogs as being German Shepherds or some other large-breed dogs, Bill told us the story about how Smoky was a notable 4-pound exception to this definition. She helped run wires and cables in places inaccessible to the troops; for example, she pulled a string with phone wires attached through 70 feet of an 8-inch pipe under a landing strip, doing a job in two minutes that would have otherwise required days of digging and exposure of Allied airplanes to the enemy.

Now, I suppose that I'd have to say that their helping the Allies win World War II had a significant impact on my (eventual) life, but Smoky and Bill just may have been responsible for everything that I am doing today in the world of therapy dogs. This detail didn't come out in the TV show, but Bill told me the whole story recently.

It began during the war, in 1944, when Bill was hospitalized with dengue fever at the 233rd Station Hospital in Nadzab, New Guinea. Bill's buddies brought him his mail, and they also brought Smoky to cheer Bill up. Two nurses saw Smoky and asked Bill—depending on if they could get permission from their commanding officer— if he would let them take Smoky on their rounds to visit battlefield casualties that were coming in from the Biak Island invasion.

"I told them sure, and they were back in ten minutes, bubbling over, with permission from the CO to do that," Bill said.

Not only that, the nurses had gotten permission from the CO to let Smoky stay on Bill's bed overnight. So they would pick up Smoky at 7 a.m., work with her all day, and then bring her back to Bill at night. They took care of all of her needs.

"I had always wondered about that CO," Bill told me. "He had to be a doctor, but he had the compassion and the vision to allow a dog to visit the injured troops in the hospital and sleep overnight on my bed, too."

He finally got the answer a few years ago. "I was watching the History Channel and there was a show about World War II, talking about the 233rd Station Hospital in New Guinea. It said that the hospital staff was made up of Mayo Clinic National Guard volunteers and was commanded by none other than Dr. Charles Mayo himself, then an Army major."

What a great endorsement for therapy dogs. In my world, I give extra credit for the compassion and vision of the medical professionals in understanding what we do with our dogs, and today we can see that these traits have apparently served Dr. Mayo quite well, indeed.

After seeing Smoky work in the battlefield hospitals, Bill realized that this could be her calling. For as long as they were in the war in the South Pacific—an additional eighteen months in combat—Bill brought Smoky to the Army and Navy hospitals regularly to visit and lift the spirits of the troops injured in battle.

Bill taught Smoky an array of tricks, and she would entertain the troops long before Bob Hope could get there. Bill used airplane parts to build a scooter and to create a "high wire" act, and he taught her to run be-tween his legs, jump through hoops and over obstacles, play dead, climb ladders, and weave through pickets. Smoky helped everyone pass the time, and she helped to settle a lot of anxieties.

After the war, Bill and Smoky returned to Cleveland and went into show business for ten years, with Smoky performing her tricks learned in the South Pacific for appreciative audiences. They continued to visit hospi-tals and the troops in Smoky's adopted home country, doing so for twelve years. At the same time, Bill worked as a professional photographer; he had a thirty-one-year career with the *Cleveland Plain Dealer* and spent more than ten years working on NASA research programs.

On this day, on Fox News with me, Bill was a great interview, and *Yorkie Doodle Dandy* was a great story. And, as I came to realize several years later, I was hear-ing the story of what was probably the first recognized therapy dog, Smoky. If I had been into therapy dogs at the time of this show like I am now, I would have happily pointed that out then.

Since I didn't do it then, I am doing it now. Bill Wynne and Smoky shaped my world.

Near the end of the interview, I told Bill that my dad had been in the South Pacific during the war—what a coincidence—and that I was happy to hear his story. "Thanks for all that you guys did for all of us."

"What did your dad do in the South Pacific?" Bill asked me.

"He flew a P-38 on photo recon," I answered. "He was in the Philippines, in the 26th Photo Recon."

Bill lit up. "That was my unit! What was your dad's name?"

"Jerry Frei."

"I knew your dad!"

Oh my God. Here it was, more than fifty years later, and suddenly I felt like I was in the Philippines, listening to two old soldiers talk about the war. They were both modest and self-effacing of what they had done for our country, as so many of that "Greatest Generation" were. After hearing Bill's Smoky stories and remembering my dad's stories about flying in the war, I can see in my mind the aerial photo taken of Dad's plane as he piloted his last mission.

When I finished the show, I ran to the telephone and called my dad, and I told him the Smoky story.

"I knew that dog, and I knew Bill. Great dog, great guy," Dad said. "I remember all of those things that he told you about."

I knew that Dad had a couple of close Army friends that he had corresponded with after they returned home, but he told me that he had not been in touch with Bill. So I put them together, and my dad, for the first time, went to a reunion of the 26th Photo Recon Squadron the following summer. There, he had some time with Bill and a lot of other old friends that had been in the war with them.

All of that made it well worth my while to have put up with a doggy wedding and snakes and birds and other stuff during my run on *Pet News* just to know that I was able to reunite the two of them.

In 2007, my friend Susan Bahary was a special guest of the Yorkshire Terrier Club of America's national specialty in New York on Westminster weekend. Susan was a longtime friend of mine from the Afghan Hound world, a great artist and sculptor, and I had followed her success in her artistic accomplishments. She called me and invited me to stop by the annual dinner at the New Yorker Hotel, as she had someone that she wanted me to meet. That was easy for me to do; I was staying at the New Yorker and heading out for dinner, so I could easily drop in.

When I got there, I was surprised to see Bill Wynne. Bill had apparently told Susan the story about him and my dad. She thought it would be nice to get us together again and didn't tell either of us of her plan. It was a nice reunion. We spoke about my father, who had passed away six years earlier.

Later that week, Bill paid me a wonderful compliment, one that I will always treasure. As part of our Westminster preshow publicity effort, I had appeared on the *Today Show* with some of our entered dogs. Bill saw the segment and sent me an email telling me, "I saw a lot of your father in you."

On Veterans Day in 2005, a memorial bronze sculpture of Smoky, created by Susan Bahary, was unveiled in the Cleveland Metroparks. It is beautiful, modeled after a famous photo of Smoky sitting up in Bill's combat helmet. In 2009, Bill was inducted into the Ohio Senior Citizens Hall of Fame and into the Press Club of Cleveland Journalism Hall of Fame.

In 2008, USA Network did a feature on Smoky and Bill for the Westminster telecast, with me doing the voice-over of the story of "the small dog with the giant legacy." At the end of the piece, coming back live to

Lester Holt and me in the booth, I was able to tell the story about my father's reunion with Bill. I held the 26th Photo Recon hat that Dad had left me after his death.

"This is a tribute to Bill Wynne and all of you guys and gals of the 'Greatest Generation,'" I said. "We salute you though the person of Bill Wynne and his dog, Yorkie Doodle Dandy (Smoky)."

Postscript: Bill is working on another book about Smoky, this one called *Angel in a Foxhole.*

> **"** *Just as my father did with a football, I know that I am changing people's lives with my dogs, visiting people in the street and visiting people in hospitals and other health care facilities.* **"**

My Father, My Dogs

Part of Cheri's job at Ronald McDonald House is to serve as a liaison to all of the faith groups in our Upper East Side neighborhood. One of them, the Bethany Memorial Reformed Church, asked her to fill in for the pastor while he was away on his honeymoon in the spring of 2009.

She was asked to deliver two sermons. The second one was for Father's Day, and she decided that it would be a good idea for me to deliver that one. I declined the opportunity at first, but then, somehow, as a wife can do, she convinced me to do it. Admittedly, the Father's Day theme was more appropriate for me than for her, so I thought I would give it a shot.

In my life, I stand before a TV camera that puts me in front of millions of people, and I have gotten to the point where that doesn't make me too nervous anymore. But standing in a pulpit in front of a congregation is a whole 'nother story. However, as I worked to put together my presentation, I started to welcome the opportunity to share my father with someone on this Father's Day.

Good morning. My name is David Frei. I am happy to be a part of this wonderful Father's Day service here at Bethany Memorial Reformed Church.

I always welcome the chance to talk about my father, Jerry Frei. I was—and I still am—quite proud of him as my father, my mentor, and my friend.

My father died in 2001. He lived in Denver, and at the time, I lived in Seattle. I got to Denver shortly after he passed, and I spent time with my mother and my siblings—one brother, three sisters—at the family home in the time between his passing and his memorial service.

One morning, I was on the coffee run for all of us, and when I pulled into the driveway on my return, I saw a fox in the front yard. I had never seen a fox here, and when I told Mom about it, she said that Dad had seen the fox once before.

I am not sure that he was aware of this—I never heard him talk about it—but the Native American Indians were great believers in animal totems. Animals would reveal themselves to you, and their spirits would then become a totem in your life, providing an awareness of personality traits in your own spiritual identity.

According to Native American Indian lore, the fox is a symbol of wisdom and is the protector of the family unit, charged with keeping the family together and safe. That was certainly my father.

So as did my father before me, I have now had a fox reveal itself to me. It makes sense to me that this would be my father's totem; the fox may have even been my father, telling me that everything would be all right. In any case, I now can carry on.

There is a country song that has the lyrics, "I am my father's son, I am inclined to do what he has done." The Bible (Proverbs 20:7) says it like this:

A righteous man who walks in his integrity, how blessed are his sons after him.

I am indeed blessed. My father was a man of integrity, and he was a spiritual man; at one point in his life he actually contemplated going to seminary. Instead, he became a football coach at the high school, college, and professional levels.

God shaped his life, and God helped him to shape the lives of others: the young people that he coached for more than fifty years.

He was a bit famous in his lifetime, but as an American poet once said, it doesn't matter who he was, what matters is who I remember he was.

I was on the *Today Show* a few years ago, right after he passed, and a man named Bill Wynne [see chapter 16] saw me. I met Bill through my involvement with dogs, and in an amazing coincidence, we discovered that he been stationed with my father in the same Army Air Corps company in the South Pacific in World War II.

Bill sent me an email that I treasure: "I just watched you on the *Today Show*, and I saw a lot of your father in you." I couldn't have had a greater compliment.

My father didn't tell me or my brother and my sisters what to think; by living his life the way he did, he showed us how to think. My father never put any pressure on me to live up to any standards, but he inspired me to be the best that I could be, to give something back to the world. He did that for others, too, teaching us that we were accountable for our actions, but he let us learn about ourselves to live productive lives and enjoy the people around us. What perfect thoughts for us on Father's Day.

My dad lived this life with a football. I am trying to live the same life with my dogs, inspired by God and inspired by my own father. My father may be gone from this world, but he lives on in my heart and in my mind and, hopefully, in the things that I do every day.

As a football coach, my dad did it with some very simple rules, rules that applied not only to his players but also to life in general. And I am finding that my dogs play by my dad's rules:

- It doesn't matter if you make a mistake, as long as you are going full speed. That means that if you are trying to do the right thing and it doesn't work out, it's OK. It's the effort and the intent that matter. This is great—my dogs are always going at full speed, living life in the fast lane.

His other rules don't need any explanation, and I can see and hear them coming from my dogs' actions:

- Be nice to people.

- Expect the best from people. They are generally good; enjoy them in your life.
- Smile.

That's a perfect fit under the heading "Unconditional Love" when it comes to dogs.

Just as my father did with a football, I know that I am changing people's lives with my dogs, visiting people in the street and visiting people in hospitals and other health care facilities. Again to Proverbs, this time 4:11–13:

I instruct you in the way of wisdom and lead you along straight paths. When you walk, your steps will not be hampered. When you run, you will not stumble. Hold on to instruction, do not let it go. Guard it well, for it is your life.

And even more from Proverbs (23:15–16):

My son, if your heart is wise, then my heart will be glad; my inmost being will rejoice when your lips speak what is right.

I hope that every day my Holy Father and my own father are looking down on me here and rejoicing.

Happy Father's Day, Dad. I love you.

Thank you all for allowing me to share my father with you. I hope that you will all celebrate this special day with my father and me.

CHAPTER 18

The End

The editors of *Dogs in Review*, a magazine of the dog show world, were running a questionnaire feature as part of their fifteenth-anniversary celebration, and they asked me to participate.

The final question was this: If Heaven exists, what would you like to hear God say when you arrive at the Pearly Gates?

My answer: "You're arriving later than we expected, but your Brittanys, Teigh and Belle, are still waiting right here for you."

I know that they will be there, along with any of my other dogs who have gone before me.

From Job 12:10:

In whose hand is the soul of every living thing, and the breath of all mankind.